Teach For America and the Struggle for Urban School Reform

Educational
PSYCHOLOGY

Critical Pedagogical Perspectives

Greg S. Goodman, *General Editor*

Vol. 21

The Educational Psychology series is part of the Peter Lang Education list.
Every volume is peer reviewed and meets
the highest quality standards for content and production.

PETER LANG
New York • Washington, D.C./Baltimore • Bern
Frankfurt • Berlin • Brussels • Vienna • Oxford

Katherine Crawford-Garrett

Teach For America and the Struggle for Urban School Reform

Searching for Agency in an Era of Standardization

PETER LANG
New York • Washington, D.C./Baltimore • Bern
Frankfurt • Berlin • Brussels • Vienna • Oxford

KH

Library of Congress Cataloging-in-Publication Data

Crawford-Garrett, Katherine.
Teach For America and the struggle for urban school reform:
Searching for agency in an era of standardization / Katherine Crawford-Garrett.
pages ; cm. — (Educational psychology: critical pedagogical perspectives; v. 21)
Includes bibliographical references.
1. Education, Urban—United States. 2. Educational change—United States.
3. School improvement programs—United States.
4. Teach For America (Project) I. Title.
LC5131.C73 370.9173'2—dc23 2013013001
ISBN 978-1-4331-2378-8 (hardcover)
ISBN 978-1-4331-2377-1 (paperback)
ISBN 978-1-4539-1151-8 (e-book)
ISSN 1943-8109

Bibliographic information published by **Die Deutsche Nationalbibliothek**.
Die Deutsche Nationalbibliothek lists this publication in the "Deutsche
Nationalbibliografie"; detailed bibliographic data is available
on the Internet at http://dnb.d-nb.de/.

The paper in this book meets the guidelines for permanence and durability
of the Committee on Production Guidelines for Book Longevity
of the Council of Library Resources.

∞

© 2013 Peter Lang Publishing, Inc., New York
29 Broadway, 18th floor, New York, NY 10006
www.peterlang.com

Printed in the United States of America

10/6/14

Table of Contents

Acknowledgments

There are so many people who helped bring this book into being. While I am listed as the sole author, I want to acknowledge that this book reflects the efforts and dedication of so many smart and talented people. I want to begin by thanking everyone at Peter Lang Publishing, especially my editor, Greg Goodman, for believing in this book and making the editorial and publication process so smooth and seamless. The guidance and encouragement that I've received have been truly exceptional.

To my colleague and friend Cathrene Connery, thank you for your mentorship and generosity. Your guidance has made the publication of this book possible. And to all of my colleagues at Ithaca College, thank you for your support and encouragement. I feel honored to have such thoughtful and dynamic associates.

I'd also like to thank my dissertation committee at the University of Pennsylvania including Gerald Campano, Kathy Schultz and Vivian Gadsden, whose wisdom and insights helped me delve deeper into my own understandings. To Susan Lytle, my advisor and dissertation chair, thank you for giving so generously to this project. Thank you for your close readings, for your hard questions, for your unfailing faith in the importance of this story and my ability to tell it. I cannot express how much your mentorship and friendship have meant to me.

Thank you to my close friends and colleagues Rachel Throop, Heather Curl, Kathleen Riley, Marlena Reese, Lee Gayle and Jenny Smith for talking me through tough moments, challenging my perspectives, inspiring me with your own work and serving as intellectual partners. To my husband, Bryan, it is impossible to adequately thank you. You have always been my biggest fan and your unwavering belief in my abilities has made all the difference.

And of course at the heart of this work are the teachers who chose to share their stories with me. The first year of teaching is never easy and I deeply respect your willingness to speak openly and with vulnerability about your experiences. I hope that your honesty, insights and critiques will be read widely, taken seriously and used to inform the landscape of educational reform in this country.

Chapter 1

THERE IS NO SINGLE STORY: PROBLEMATIZING THE AMERICAN SCHOOL REFORM NARRATIVE

In September 2005 I took a leave of absence from my teaching position to spend the year in the Democratic Republic of Congo where my boyfriend was working in the humanitarian aid industry. The eastern part of the country was in the midst of a complicated, ten-year conflict characterized by rogue militias, rampant rape and the pillage of natural resources. As I arrived via a Red Cross flight from Kenya, I braced myself for outward manifestations of the violence—burned-out shells of buildings, dazed inhabitants maimed by machete, orphaned children roaming the streets. My suitcase held $1200 in cash, a bar of soap and an odd collection of clothes and books. But that was not all that I brought. I also carried a simple narrative about the war that cast the Rwandans as perpetrators, the Congolese as victims and the foreign aid workers as noble helpers—a story circulated widely by the Western media outlets to which I subscribed. As Chimamanda Adichie (2009) asserts, "So that is how to create a single story, show people as one thing, as only one thing, over and over again, and that is what they become."

While I clung fiercely to this narrative during my first weeks in country, I soon began to bump up against conflicting accounts. I was surprised, for example, to overhear the aid workers derisively assert that "the Congolese can't do anything." I lived in a walled compound guarded by two Congolese men, neither of whom was permitted to come indoors. One afternoon, I met a Belgian woman who spoke brazenly about the business opportunities her husband had discovered amidst the destruction. A disgruntled taxi driver taking me across the border to Rwanda lectured me at length on the beauty of Rwanda's roads and by extension the superiority of its people. I found myself taking photos of street kids, only to be scolded harshly by nearby adults. I should have known better; there was so much I didn't understand.

Jason Stearns is a young white American whose book *Dancing in the Glory of Monsters* (2011) attempts to explain the nuances of Congo's war. His interviewees were wary of his agenda and doubtful that, as an outsider, he could produce an accurate narrative. Considering the ways in which problematic depictions of Congo have previously engendered serious consequences, they had a right to be concerned. In 1994, for example, Western nations set up a vast network of camps in eastern Congo in order to ease the suffering of refugees fleeing the violence in neighboring Rwanda. This move was partly a response to media coverage that horrified the Western world—scenes which included a cholera epidemic, mass starvation and small children with machete wounds to the skull. Yet, as it turns out, the camps did not serve the purpose that Western donors had first envisioned. Instead of providing for destitute refugees, the camps also housed the perpetrators of the genocide, allowing them to re-arm and wreak havoc on the surrounding communities. Thus the story was more complicated than it first seemed and the mandate, which sounded so simple in the beginning—dole out food and medicine to those in need—ultimately prolonged a conflict that continues today and has claimed the lives of nearly 5 million people (Polman, 2011; Stearns, 2011).

In those days, I never paused to consider the parallels that might exist between the urban classroom and my time in Congo. But when I entered graduate school to study urban schooling in the United States, I found Congo still present to me—periodically pushing at the edges of my mind. There were times when I would be reading about the current education reform efforts and hear echoes of central Africa. Just as my understandings of Congo became more nuanced and complicated, I found that my narratives of urban schooling underwent a parallel evolution. The casualties, obviously, were quite different but the similarities were undeniable—the same interlocking accounts of hope and frustration, the same noble instinct to address injustice, the same complexity hidden beneath a guise of simplicity, the same one-size-fits-all solutions, the same cycle of intensity and burnout, the same power differential, the same reliance on a single story to explain a multiplicity of perspectives, the same intractable problem persisting like the strain of a rare disease, stubbornly immune to even the most robust and innovative treatments. The urban classroom, like Congo, "has always defied the idealists" (Stearns, 2011, p. 9).

I begin with this metaphor in part to suggest that the mainstream media accounts of current education reform efforts not only re-inscribe the pervasive stereotypes of teachers and students, but also fail to adequately address the complexities of the proposed solutions. Within such accounts, schools of education are typically portrayed as encumbrances to reform while organizations like Teach For America (TFA) and charter school networks like KIPP,[1] which advocate for the de-regulation of teacher preparation, are heralded as harbingers of much-needed change (Cochran-Smith & Fries, 2001). Furthermore, the tragedy of urban education in this country has become a media spectacle, with the film *Waiting for Superman* garnering accolades, regardless of its limiting portrayals of teachers, optimistic endorsement of school choice and unexamined claim that outside intervention is an unequivocal good (Miner, 2010). As a result, donors with little educational expertise, like hedge fund managers and investment bankers, are showing interest in school reform by sponsoring charter schools and extolling an accountability agenda despite the critiques of veteran teachers and education scholars (Miner, 2010; Ravitch, 2010). In her critical reconsideration of the standards movement, Ravitch (2010), for example, notes the troubling outcomes that have resulted from an overemphasis on high-stakes testing. These critiques, however scathing, have had little impact on popular conceptions of urban education. Like disasters abroad, which periodically capture the world's attention (Polman, 2011), urban schooling has become the cause célèbre of philanthropists in the United States, or what Arne Duncan has referred to as "the civil rights issue of our generation" (as quoted in Dillon, 2009). The favored remedies, however, have little to do with the deep, reflective and locally driven approach that characterized the Civil Rights movement, emphasizing instead the de-professionalization of teachers, the persistent depiction of students and families as deficient and an overreliance on top-down mechanisms to improve teaching and learning.

Often at the center of discussions about school reform is Teach For America, whose corps members make a number of personal and professional sacrifices to commit two years of their lives to teaching in impoverished urban and rural settings across America. With little formal background in education and an accompanying dearth of extensive preparation, corps members, like aid workers in Congo, begin to embody the tension they encounter as they try to do good work and improve the life chances of their students in the face of significant adversity.

---

1 KIPP stands for the Knowledge Is Power Program, a nationwide network of urban charter schools founded upon a "No Excuses" philosophy.

In an effort to explore and theorize these tensions, this book traces the journeys of forty-three corps members working within a "failing" school district—in an effort to consider how those teachers negotiated the dominant narrative of urban schooling in the United States, and their position within it, in order to meet the needs of their students. By attending to the analytic lenses which TFA corps members apply to their circumstances, I illustrate how these new teachers are often forced to reconcile their hopes and expectations for urban education with the reality of a system that favors compliance and obedience over ingenuity and compassion. Moreover, I consider how their socialization into the profession positions them as passive recipients of knowledge and engenders deficit ideologies of students, families and communities. As bureaucratic challenges emerged, cultural differences were revealed, and the limitations of the individual were made apparent; the corps members with whom I worked had to negotiate the requisite tensions and re-conceptualize their mission to remedy educational injustice. Like aid workers in Congo, corps members spent a significant portion of their first year in the classroom, straddling a discourse of possibility (Macedo, 1994) and a discourse of deficit (Flores, Cousin, & Diaz, 1991) as they tried to reconcile their hopes and desires for their students with institutional mandates and constraints.

I also examine my role as a teacher educator in introducing multiple educational lenses to the corps members. Specifically, I explore how the university methods course can serve as a site of productive disruption (an adaptation of the concept of "constructive disruption" as used in Cochran-Smith & Lytle, 2009) and encourage corps members to 1) critically engage with the institutional settings which shape their experiences, 2) question and problematize deficit ideologies and 3) adopt and enact identities as knowledgeable practitioners.

Data Collection

Data for this study were collected over the course of the 2010–2011 academic year in Ridgeville,[2] a post-industrial northeastern city with a population of 1.5 million people, during which time I followed a single cohort of incoming Teach For America corps members who were assigned to teach elementary school and were thus enrolled in my methods courses. Participation in the study was voluntary and out of forty-six possible participants, thirty-nine chose to participate. There were twenty-six Caucasian teachers, three of whom were male; ten African American teachers, all of whom were female; two Latina

---

2 Ridgeville is a pseudonym.

teachers; and one Asian male. I also included three second-year corps members in the study. Of these, one was a Caucasian female and two were Latino men. Of those willing to participate, twenty self-selected for more intensive participation, expressing a desire to have me conduct regular weekly visits to their classrooms and to be interviewed in one-on-one or small group settings or to participate in focus groups. Of these, I used purposeful maximal sampling (Creswell, 2007) to select a diverse group of thirteen teachers to interview and observe regularly.[3] All of these teachers were placed within the Excel Charter Network[4] and thus all of my observations and field visits took place at Excel elementary schools. During classroom visits I acted as a participant observer, taking notes and interacting with teachers and children when it felt appropriate to do so. In addition to the first-year corps members who make up the bulk of the participants in this study, I also interviewed three second-year corps members who had been my students the previous year in the hopes that they would reflect critically upon their experiences in Teach For America, the school district and their university courses. Primary data for the study included audio-recorded and transcribed class sessions; field notes from classroom visits; interview and focus-group recordings and transcripts; and documents ranging from lesson plans to student assignments to official materials disseminated by TFA, the school district and the Excel Charter Network.

Each methods course was seven weeks in length and met for two hours each Tuesday evening on the university's campus. The elementary literacy methods course occurred during the fall semester. Similarly, the social studies methods course met during the spring semester. While the courses were abbreviated in comparison to regular university courses to encourage a deep inquiry into teaching and learning, many of the course assignments extended beyond the formal dates during which the class met. Therefore, I maintained close contact with many of the corps members for much of the year, meeting and working with them on their assignments outside of class hours. Also, while "time" in and of itself is not a central factor in my analysis, it is important to note that because I encountered corps members at different points throughout the year, I was able to observe and document some degree of change as corps members contended with readings, ideas and assignments at distinct and varied points in their classroom journeys.

---

3 When I use the term "corps member" henceforth in this book, I am only referring to those specific corps members who participated in this research study, not corps members generally.
4 Excel is a pseudonym.

Features of the Course

Because the course was specifically framed as an inquiry, a significant amount of course time each week was devoted to corps members working collaboratively in inquiry groups in which they shared problematic aspects of their practice, discussed course readings, planned curriculum and analyzed policy. These inquiry groups remained the same over the course of the academic year with the expectation that corps members would develop close relationships with one another and that the inquiry groups would function as spaces of deep learning and collaboration.

Moreover, these groups also served as a platform from which to challenge the isolating aspects of teaching and learning. For example, corps members shared some or all of their written assignments with members of their inquiry groups—either by reading excerpts aloud in class or posting assignments to a Google group online in order to solicit feedback. The assignments themselves were designed to be tied closely to the classroom practice of the teachers and to provide opportunities for corps members to explicitly engage with students. For example, the literacy course included an interview assignment in which corps members were required to spend time talking to students about their in- and out-of-school literacy practices. Further, curricular assignments such as a literacy lesson plan and social studies unit invited corps members to experiment with curriculum and pedagogy and were thus meant to enhance the kinds of interactions that occurred on a daily basis between corps members and their students. While most corps members had become accustomed to relying solely upon direct instruction to introduce, convey and assess content, course assignments generally asked them to reconsider this mode of instruction and to introduce a range of pedagogical techniques.

Another salient feature of the course that bears mentioning up front is the content of the course readings that focused thematically on issues of difference and, in so doing, attempted to acknowledge and problematize issues of equity within urban schools. In selecting readings for the course, I intentionally selected pieces that depicted minority communities from an asset-based perspective. I also aimed to offer rich portraits of urban teaching and learning and, in so doing, to portray urban teachers as knowledgeable practitioners capable of generating knowledge in their field. Finally, I explicitly chose readings that both complicated and broadened mainstream definitions of literacy, with the expectation that alternative conceptions of literacy would naturally lead to more expansive instructional practices.

Data Analysis

I drew upon two methodological orientations as a means for data analysis: ethnographic methods and practitioner research. The unit of analysis varied in accordance with the types of data collected and approach to analysis selected; documents produced by TFA or Excel, for example, reflect institutional norms and procedures while classroom discussions and one-on-one interviews encourage a more localized analysis of a group or an individual.

Ethnographic Methods

While the proposed study was not lengthy or immersive enough to be categorized as a traditional ethnography, I approached my data from an "ethnographic perspective." With regards to ethnographic research in the field of education, Green and Bloome (1997) state that "central to an ethnographic perspective is the use of theories of culture and inquiry practices derived from anthropology or sociology to guide the research" (p. 183). By adopting an ethnographic perspective, I chose to consider these teachers not merely as individuals but also as members of particular groups who share certain experiences and practices. Their affiliation with Teach For America or Excel, for example, implies a shared set of cultural practices and beliefs worthy of exploration. Because the study was multi-sited and required, in accordance, that I enact a wide range of researcher positionalities, conducting a traditional ethnographic study was unfeasible. Taking an ethnographic perspective, instead, allowed me to draw upon those ethnographic methods of data analysis most pertinent to my project, including thick description, coding and theme generation.

Practitioner Research

Because this study focused on not only generating knowledge but also influencing practice, the action research cycle of "plan, act, observe, reflect" was a critical component of my ongoing data analysis (Herr & Anderson, 2005, p. 5). While action research has numerous faces and iterations, emphasis is always placed on transparency within the research process. In this sense, data analysis cannot be conceived of as a practice done in isolation or a task to complete once the project is finished; rather, analysis in my study had to be ongoing, recursive and central to the methods course itself. In other words, the analysis I engaged in as part of the action research cycle affected the direction of the course, the kinds of conversations and discussions I had with my students and, ultimately, the ways I chose to explore the research questions I have posed within this study. In particular, at points during the course when corps members seemed frustrated by class activities or expressed interest in topics not covered by the syllabus, I altered the direction of the course in the hopes of making it more meaningful and relevant. I considered these points in the course "critical" incidents or generative moments and tried, when possible, to use these moments as starting points for deeper inquiry into particular areas of interest.

Theoretical Frames for Analysis

My approach to analysis was inspired by Lather's (1991) text *Getting Smart: Feminist Research and Pedagogy with/in the Postmodern*, in which she attempts to interrupt positivist research paradigms by crafting a series of narrative vignettes that tell four different stories about her data set. By drawing upon realist, critical, deconstructive and self-reflexive lenses to illuminate various aspects of data collected from an introductory women's studies course, Lather aptly demonstrates the limitations of attempting to use data to tell a single story. In a similar analytic move, I draw upon an array of theoretical frameworks in an effort to add nuance and complexity to the narrative of urban school reform. At different points in this analysis, for example, I utilize 1) Foucauldian notions of discipline and power to highlight the ways in which corps members both experience and internalize the mechanisms of control exerted by their respective schools; 2) international humanitarianism to illustrate the complexity that accompanies a desire to help others and to remedy inequities; 3) conceptions of knowledge and practice within teaching and learning; and 4) critical, collaborative feminist research which foregrounds and complicates notions of empowerment and illustrates the potential of collaborative inquiry to invite new perspectives. The application of these contrastive frameworks allows for unique insight into various facets of the data and further contributes to a more nuanced understanding of what it means to undertake urban teaching in these times (Lytle, 2006). Moreover, these frameworks suggest the sense of reciprocity that was manifest in the data analysis process. As emic terms emerged during class discussions, written assignments, focus groups or interviews, these terms, in a number of cases, became analytic frames which were then used to theorize broader themes. For example, a number of corps members drew upon the notion of "Taylorism" (discussed at length in Chapter 3) as a way to explain their experiences in the school district or the Excel Charter Network and thus Taylorism became an important mode of analysis primarily because it was meaningful to the study's participants.

By positioning myself as a critically conscious researcher as Lather (1991) does, I recognize that knowledge is always situated, partial and mediated through the lens of the researcher. Further, I acknowledge the complexity of asking the students in my courses to participate in my research and recognize that they may have felt pressure to contribute more extensively to my project as a result of my position of authority (LeCompte, 1994). I do not assume, then, that this study will produce some enduring truth or single story about the ways in which TFA corps members make sense of their experiences in urban communities and classrooms. Rather, I adopt a postmodern stance, one which seeks to recognize a multitude of possible "truths" (Lyotard, 1979). Further, while certain qualitative methodologies, particularly action research, are viewed as hopelessly subjective and therefore flawed, I contend, like others (Cochran-Smith & Lytle, 1993; Herr & Anderson, 2005), that practitioners can and do generate essential knowledge about education; that this knowledge is often disseminated through stories about teaching and learning; and that these narratives inspire teachers to draw parallels to their own classrooms, reconsider dilemmas of practice and alter their approaches accordingly (Herr & Anderson, 2005).

Researcher Positionality

My own positionality as a teacher and researcher undoubtedly played a significant role in the kinds of data that were collected, how the data were analyzed and the book that was produced as a result. At different points, I functioned as a professor, confidante, mentor, friend and supervisor. In some cases these multiple and shifting roles engendered a sense of intimacy, understanding and companionship, though in other instances they led to conflict and frustration, phenomena which will be analyzed further in Chapter 6.

In describing the complex and highly reflexive nature of ethnography, Richardson (1997) writes, "I am the field which I never leave" (p. 4). Because we inevitably take our "selves" into whichever research site we enter, being aware of our multiple subjectivities takes on increased urgency and I spent considerable time reflecting on my own positionality. My experience as a former elementary school teacher was one that significantly shaped my approach to this study and to my students. I began my career at a progressive charter school located in a diverse and gentrifying neighborhood of Washington, DC. While many of the challenges I faced in my first several years of teaching mirror those faced by the TFA corps members in my methods courses, my early experiences in the classroom were also unique; the administrative staff at my school never questioned or attempted to manipulate the curricular decisions I made as a teacher. In fact, they encouraged the development of thematic units of study which would be meaningful to students, locally compelling and reflective of larger, global issues. While this location allows me to view urban education from a platform of possibility, having viewed firsthand the types of rich learning opportunities which can and do emerge from such environments, it also inhibits, on some level, my ability to understand the very real constraints the corps members experience as novice educators in an increasingly rigid public school district. Faced with the dual pressures of declining test scores and chronic budget deficits, these teachers are afforded little, if any, space to design or imagine alternate experiences for their students.

While the kinds of pedagogy and curriculum I was permitted to use set me distinctly apart from the corps members, I am not entirely unfamiliar with their teaching contexts. As part of my graduate assistantship, I served as a mentor for two years to first-year corps members, a role which entailed making classroom visits, meeting to plan curriculum, exchanging ideas about teaching and learning via email and providing substantive and, at times, evaluative feedback when required. Over time, I came to realize the importance of the relational aspects of this work and subsequently spent more time with corps members outside of their school contexts and less time trying to evaluate and assess their teaching. In doing this work, I became increasingly aware of the kinds of narratives teachers constructed about their teaching, classrooms and students. Specifically, corps members seemed to be wrestling with issues of poverty and inequality and I found that these themes were often subtexts of our more straightforward conversations about teaching and learning.

Race and class are two additional aspects of my positionality that significantly shaped this work. As a white, upper-middle-class woman who has spent the bulk of my career attempting to teach across racial, cultural and socioeconomic lines, I find that I must continually re-visit and re-consider the ways in which these gendered, classed and raced ways of knowing and being influence the work I do with both teachers and students. While I have created syllabi, lesson plans and discussion questions that aim to represent a range of perspectives, particularly those outside of the mainstream, I acknowledge that my positionality as a member of the dominant culture means that inevitable blind spots will impede my curricular selections, pedagogical practices and interactions with these teachers. However, the privileges I enjoy due to my position within the dominant culture overlap and intersect with the privileges enjoyed by many of the corps members I teach (though certainly not all). Therefore, my stories of teaching in a diverse, urban school became classroom texts—ones which I tried to use not to reinforce notions of expertise but to expose, unpack and critique my own classroom practice. Like Kamler (2001), I sought to invite my students to work alongside me as we wrestled with how "narratives are told, how they are made, how they might be written differently, how they support, undermine and struggle with other stories, how their writing affects both the teller and the told" (p. 46).

Organization of the Book

This book is organized around a set of broad, overlapping themes which emerged from the data set and which collectively form a vivid picture of how new teachers contend with the dominant narrative of urban reform in the face of the diverse needs of their urban students and their own hopes and desires as urban teachers. Chapter 2 aims to situate the corps members against the current political backdrop, particularly the kinds of policies being instituted at the local and national level, including Teach For America and the charter school movement, both of which influence how corps members understand their students, the profession of teaching and their own sense of efficacy. In Chapter 3, through the application of a Foucauldian frame, I consider the relationship between innovation and obedience and explore the ways in which bureaucratic mandates significantly inhibit experimentation with classroom practice and limit the range of identities new teachers can adopt. Chapter 4 explores resonances between the field of urban education and international humanitarianism, particularly what it means for corps members to try to help their students and how this desire, however laudatory, can compromise communication and collaboration with families. I also consider how corps members come to understand their students' underachievement, where blame is assigned for educational failure and how teachers justify their own decisions to remain in or to abandon the urban classroom. Chapter 5 is primarily concerned with questions of epistemology, particularly what counts as knowledge within the field of teaching, what kinds of data are deemed credible and what modes of knowing are favored by Teach For America, charter school leaders, district officials and the corps members themselves. I also explore how an espoused lack of knowledge about teaching makes the questioning of top-down policies difficult for the corps members, even in the face of contradictory classroom evidence. Through the application of a critical, feminist, collaborative perspective, Chapter 6 seeks both to expose the inner workings of the courses I taught and to scrutinize the invitations I offered the corps members to critically reflect upon their practice. Further, I consider how my own desire to "help" these young teachers proved problematic at different junctures. Within this chapter I analyze the methods course as a genre and consider the potential it holds as a site of meaningful inquiry; in particular, I explore what it might mean to disrupt the technical view of teacher preparation which has historically socialized teachers to follow orders and to consider, instead, how the methods course could serve as a humanizing space built upon the dual pillars of collaboration and critical inquiry.

Perhaps more than anything this book reflects the complexities and tensions that urban classroom teachers must face as they attempt to negotiate a range of contrasting discourses regarding what it means to remedy longstanding educational injustice. To highlight this tension, I emphasize the voices of the teachers as they narrate their understandings and beliefs about their role within the urban educational system. Moreover, I consider my own assumptions, desires and motivations to "help" the corps members through the methods courses I taught and further explore the ways in which a helping agenda and a commitment to inquiry are at once complementary and contradictory. The goal of this text is not to suggest a state of hopelessness with regards to school reform in the United States or to imply that the complexities inherent in working for educational justice render it a doomed enterprise. Rather, I aim to illustrate that new teachers would benefit significantly from spaces that present multiple perspectives on urban education and encourage critical inquiry so that projects aimed at reform are taken up thoughtfully. Moreover, this study demonstrates that in order to engender trust, promote hope and encourage the kind of enduring change that the corps members so vigorously work towards, agency must extend beyond the offices of reform organizations and district bureaucracies to students and teachers who exist at the nexus of possibility.

Chapter 2
THE STRUGGLING URBAN DISTRICT: TEACH FOR AMERICA AND SCHOOL PRIVATIZATION

Teaching is a political endeavor and schools, especially those under the scrutiny of district or state authorities, are highly charged political environments. The corps members I worked with entered a complicated political milieu characterized by drastic changes in school leadership within the district, the expanding presence of charter schools and decreased teacher autonomy. Thus, in addition to negotiating the organizational mandates and expectations of Teach For America, corps members also had to decipher the broader context of Ridgeville at a time when the school district was under intense pressure to reform. As a result, many found that they had to reconcile their personal convictions regarding social justice education with the moralistic and technical control exerted within their school contexts. Many struggled to reconcile the realities of their teaching environments with their hopes to inspire lasting educational change. Further, the restrictive approaches of organizations like TFA and the Excel Charter Network with whom they were closely affiliated contributed to their overall feeling of disillusionment and thus often rendered resistance unfeasible.

While many Ridgeville corps members expressed a desire to introduce new approaches to classrooms which they viewed as overly prescriptive, the constraints of current education reform initiatives made it nearly impossible to do so. This chapter thus explores the political contexts and locations that inform the experiences of Ridgeville corps members; documents how they experience the moralistic and technical control exerted by Teach For America, the district and the Excel Charter Network;[5] and illustrates that they both embrace and resist current school reform narratives regarding urban teaching and learning.

Teach For America: Background and Critiques

Just as international NGOs predicate their recruitment on the desire of young people to do meaningful work in the world, TFA seeks corps members who are willing to work relentlessly to close the achievement gap. According to the organization's website, Teach For America's mission is "to grow the movement of leaders who work to ensure that kids growing up in poverty get an excellent education" (www.teachforamerica.org). In order to accomplish this, TFA "enlists committed individuals, invests in leaders and accelerates impact." Teach For America frames corps members' initial two-year commitment as the beginning of a longer career that might lead into other sectors but will be characterized by an ongoing commitment to working for educational equity, no matter the ultimate sector of employment. There is no shortage of recent college graduates willing to take on this work. In fact, despite mixed results on quantitative measures aiming to assess the effectiveness of its teachers (Boyd, Grossman, Lankford, Loeb, & Wyckoff, 2006), TFA continues to garner nationwide attention, attracting an increasingly competitive pool of applicants from the nation's most elite colleges. TFA has become the nation's largest provider of teachers to low-income communities and the network of alumni and corps members is over 17,000 strong, and growing. Moreover, between 2000 and 2008, Teach For America received more than $213 million in grant money, far more than any other single organization in the United States (Fairbanks, 2011). Although the reach and prestige of the program have continued to expand, little scholarly attention has been paid to the experience of the corps members themselves, who, despite their varied accomplishments, contend daily with a number of significant challenges. Not only are these teachers placed in geographic areas that are often unfamiliar to them, they also have a dearth of formal training in education, having completed only a five-week summer training institute. Most important, perhaps, TFA corps members are expected to meet

---

4 While TFA, the Ridgeville School District and the Excel Charter Network are all separate entities with distinct philosophies and approaches to improving student achievement, significant overlap does exist in their approaches to teacher preparation, behavior management and monitoring student achievement; thus, at times they are listed and referenced collectively.

the academic needs of a diverse student body; negotiate a number of strict curricular mandates; and, in most cases, mediate a range of cultural, racial and socioeconomic differences between them and their students.

Though now an established form of entry into the teaching profession, TFA continues to face criticism on a number of fronts; the two most persistent critiques concern the relative preparedness of its teachers to enter urban and rural communities and the short commitment they are asked to make to those settings. Several former corps members have published accounts of their first year of teaching that lament their lack of preparedness and its impact on their students (Hopkins, 2008; Schorr, 1993). In his open letter to former president Bill Clinton concerning proposed revisions to the TFA model, Jonathan Schorr (1993) confesses that he "—like most TFAers—harbored dreams of liberating [his] students from public school mediocrity and offering them as good an education as [he] had received" (p. 317). According to Schorr, this unexamined idealism rendered him an ineffective teacher who was ultimately unable to reach his students. In a similar piece critiquing her induction into teaching, Megan Hopkins (2008) states that she entered the classroom without possessing a "deep understandings of or appreciation for the experiences of my students or their community" (p. 4), an oversight which she considers one of the most problematic of her Teach For America preparation. Perhaps in response to the above critique, TFA has taken a more active role in pursuing partnerships with schools of education to expand the kinds of experiences and support that corps members will be offered during their two-year tenure (Koerner, Lynch, & Martin, 2008).

While these programmatic changes and alliances with more traditional forms of teacher preparation have quelled some of the criticism of TFA, education advocates continue to voice concerns regarding the brief commitment which TFA teachers make to their urban and rural placements. Historically, TFA has countered this critique by insisting that the goal of the organization is not to prepare lifelong teachers but rather to give future leaders an indelible experience in urban and rural settings which will significantly affect their lives, no matter the career path they ultimately choose: "Our alumni are a powerful and growing force for change. By exerting leadership from inside and outside education, our nearly 17,000 alumni leverage their corps experience to improve outcomes and opportunities for low-income students and to fight for systemic reform" (www.teachforamerica.org).

However, in a recent study conducted to gauge the level of civic involvement of former corps members, McAdams and Brandt (2009) found that TFA corps members who completed their two-year commitment actually reported less civic involvement than either those who dropped out of the program midway through or those who were initially accepted into the program but chose not to matriculate. In positing potential reasons for this disparity, McAdams and Brandt (2009) contend that the students' encounters in urban and rural high-poverty schools could have proved "sufficiently disillusioning to dissuade them from future service" (p. 955). Moreover, teachers who completed their classroom tenure in urban rather than rural placements report more negative feelings regarding the TFA experience as a whole. Not surprisingly, those teachers who reported a dearth of support and a lack of efficacy had the most negative impressions of their participation in TFA years after the experience. Trends such as these are not only disturbing; they also provide a compelling rationale for attempting to understand how these teachers are socialized to enter the teaching profession and the ways in which they make sense of urban communities in which they work, as their localized experiences have broader implications for teacher preparation, efficacy and retention.

Perhaps because TFA's stated mission is "to eliminate educational inequity by enlisting our nation's most promising future leaders in the effort" (www.teachforamerica.org), most published studies on the organization have focused on test scores in an attempt to assess whether TFA teachers have been successful in closing the achievement gap. Unfortunately, the majority of these studies (Boyd et al., 2006; Darling-Hammond, Holtzman, Gatlin, & Heilig, 2005; Decker, Mayer, & Glazerman, 2004; Laczko-Kerr & Berliner, 2002) tell us little regarding the actual experiences of corps members and their students; in particular, no one addresses how corps members come to understand the inequities they mean to address.

In an early but still relevant study of the organization, Popkewitz (1998) spent the first academic year of TFA's existence (1991–1992) interviewing corps members and conducting ethnographic fieldwork with a particular focus on the ways in which the teachers discursively "construct" the urban and rural child. His findings illustrate that many of the teachers' pedagogical and curricular decisions are guided by unstated white, middle-class norms which consistently cast the urban/rural student as "other." When a teacher spoke of a child's potential for example, Popkewitz argued that she was essentially recasting a child's negative or pathological qualities and thereby positioning herself as savior able to draw out and actualize a child's hidden assets and intellect. In this sense the child can never be normal or average but remains trapped in what Popkewitz refers to as an "oppositional space" (p. 56).

An outspoken advocate for teacher education and professionalization, Darling-Hammond (1994) shares Popkewitz's concerns. In an article also produced during the early days of the organization, she attempts to illustrate the ways in which Teach For America functions problematically in the lives of students, arguing that "good intentions that fail to produce good teaching for African American and Latino children look like a thin veil for arrogance, condescension, and continuing neglect" (pp. 22–23). Like Popkewitz, she likens TFA to a missionary organization, one in which the teachers are framed as saviors of poor, urban and rural schoolchildren. Darling-Hammond further contends that unprepared beginning teachers blame the students rather than themselves for the perceived challenges and struggles, a tendency which has contributed to instances of racial tension among teachers, parents and students.

As alternative teacher certification programs like TFA continue to capture the national imagination and reinforce narratives of social mobility through education, it becomes increasingly important to consider the ways in which teachers within these programs make sense of their mission. The corps members highlighted in this study, for example, actively sought spaces in which to discuss, complicate and critique their roles within urban communities. Moreover, because TFA teachers are positioned via the organization to enter leadership roles in a variety of settings after completing their tenure as classroom teachers, it becomes even more urgent to consider the conceptions of teaching and learning that former corps members will carry into these settings, how these conceptions might influence future decision-making and the ways in which certain understandings can work for and against TFA's mission to provide an excellent education for all students. Thus far, issues of educational equity with regards to TFA have been considered primarily through the lens of testing outcomes; how teachers experience, discuss and make sense of the inequities they encounter remains a largely undertheorized area.

The Local Context

The 2010–2011 corps members arrived in Ridgeville at a time when the school district was implementing a dramatic new reform initiative aimed at addressing chronically low-performing schools. In an effort to remedy consistently failing schools, the district introduced a new initiative which allowed charter and contract organizations to bid for control of select district schools; the district promised an increased amount of autonomy in exchange for rigorous accountability. Parents and community members were explicitly invited to offer input into the redevelopment of the school through the implementation of advisory councils set up by the school district. Some of the turnaround schools remained under district control. These schools instituted significant staffing changes, an extended school day and year and the adoption of a tightly controlled, highly scripted curriculum in both reading and math. Those schools taken over by charter organizations were subject to even more drastic changes as charter companies attempted to build schools which reflected their own educational philosophies. One of the most pervasive charter networks in Ridgeville is the Excel Charter Network, which manages an increasing number of middle schools and high schools under the motto "Excellence: no excuses." While charter schools based on the "no-excuses" model continue to proliferate nationwide, critics have contended that this approach to school reform conceals factors like institutional racism and systemic inequality, making true educational change impossible (Lack, 2009).

Excel added three elementary schools to its existing network of four secondary schools during the 2010–2011 school year, applying the same principles of test preparation and college readiness that the organization deemed effective at the secondary level.

Excel's stated educational philosophy resonates with that of TFA and includes an overarching sense of urgency in addressing student underachievement, a focus on identifying and utilizing the most "efficient" instructional methods and the "relentless" work of teachers towards achieving their goal of educational equity. The following excerpt from their website outlines their commitment to urban education:

> We are relentlessly committed to student achievement. We know that all students can and must achieve. Our expectations are high, our desire for success is intense and our timeline is aggressive. We use clear and concrete measures to determine achievement. When we fail, we own it and look to develop better and more effective methods. We constantly explore new strategies to increase our effectiveness and we never get hung up on pedagogical fads or ideologies. We know that high expectations must be matched by high and efficient levels of support. We are united by our shared mission, by the urgency of the calling, and by our relentless pursuit of academic achievement for all. (Organization website, retrieved June 2011)

Like the school district, Excel entered existing schools with the goal of transforming school culture and academic performance as quickly as possible. The sweeping changes to the district were not without controversy among the community at large. During the year this study took place, a citywide protest erupted when a young teacher was disciplined for resisting the takeover of her high school by a charter company and encouraging her students to do the same. The teacher was reinstated after a month of suspension but the incident brought to light the tensions surrounding school transformation in a troubled urban district and raised serious questions regarding whether schools were being offered adequate opportunities to improve their performance before undergoing significant shifts in leadership

Despite the range of approaches and providers, the schools slated to be turned around all shared one thing in common: their teaching staffs contained a considerable number of first-year TFA corps members. Nearly all of the TFA corps members taking my methods course during the 2010–2011 school year were placed either in schools managed by the Excel Charter Network or in other "failing" schools which had been taken over by the district. Thus, the schools identified as most in need of radical remedies to reinvent themselves were all at least partly staffed by first-year teachers who had little or no prior teaching experience. As Cochran-Smith and Lytle (2006) note, "It is precisely the students in these schools, who have not traditionally been well served by the system who need the best teachers but who often end up with the teachers who are least prepared" (p. 685). As a result, many of these schools relied on pre-scriptive curricula and a mandated instructional approach to accommodate a teaching staff that possessed little formal experience, an approach which is not uncommon according to Oakes, Franke, Quartz, and Rogers (2002) who assert that policy makers have typically responded to teacher shortages by "adopt[ing] highly 'prescriptive,' 'teacherproof' curricula" (p. 228). However, the authors go on to claim that these solutions accomplish little in the short run and will diminish the capacity of the teaching force for years to come.

Though the vast majority were not education majors in college, the Ridge-ville corps members featured in this account entered the local context with a wide range of experiences with U.S. school reform initiatives. A few had studied education as undergrads and expressed concerns early in the semester regarding the prospect of working at a charter school or participating in Teach For America and thus entered both contexts with skepticism and hesitation. Despite being mired in the daily logistics of the classroom, many corps members brought these broader political concerns to bear on class discussions. Daphne, for example, noted the following regarding her decision to take a position at Excel:

I talked to one of the people at TFA and I said I didn't want to take the interview because I didn't want to work at a charter school, because I have a really big problem with
it. I worked at a magnet school and I don't think the lottery system is fair, but a lot of
charter schools in Connecticut handpick kids. Morally I feel that is wrong. I want to
help the kids that don't get into the schools. They talked to me about how [Excel] is
different and all this research on [Excel] is different. They take every kid from the district and I'm like, all right. I was like, "I'm in love with [Excel]. Bring it on. I'm so
excited."

Clearly, Daphne initially had objections to charter schools, based on their
presumed selectivity but once assured that Excel did not "handpick" students,
she was open to accepting the position. Ultimately, she espoused the value that
all students have the right to a quality education but did not necessarily
recognize that, as a systemic reform, charter schools cannot possibly accommodate all of the students who wish to attend them. Erica, another corps member,
had similar sentiments when informed she was to interview with Excel:

[They told me,] "You're only interviewing with charter schools." And I was like, "I
don't want to teach at a charter school! I don't want to be a part of that. You know, I
had a lot of preconceived notions about it that probably weren't based in anything,
but—And I had my interview with [Excel], in which they were like—I had literally just
two days before I turned in a twenty-page paper on the detriments of standardized
testing—and my first question starting off in this interview was, "What do you think
about standardized testing and what do you think about using it to assess teachers?"
And I was like, "Oh my god. I can't work here." And then a week later I found out that
that's where I would be working. And I had this, like, conflict. And I had this PC answer, of being like, you know, I think there are a lot of cultural problems with standardized testing and I'd be interested in seeing how you develop your tests. . . . So it was
this identity crisis almost in a way that I had, which is dramatic for me to say I guess,
but I spent my spring semester at college being like, "Oh my god. Where am I going?
What am I doing?" And then I tried to justify it for myself, like, well, maybe [Excel] is
right. They're having a lot of success rates. Their kids are going to college. And yeah,
teachers should be held accountable. And I tried to really buy into it. And still being in
this environment, I don't feel like I'm—I feel like I'm just a cog. Like you just feel like
you are a cog at the hands of a lot of different people who want to tell you what to
believe and what to do and what is right and everyone else is wrong.

As one of the few elementary corps members in my course coming from an
education background, Erica found herself at odds with the philosophical
underpinnings of Excel and yet repeatedly discounted her own misgivings by
making statements like "You know, I had a lot of preconceived notions about it
that probably weren't based on anything, but—" or "And then I tried to justify

it for myself, like, well, maybe [Excel] is right. They're having a lot of success rates." She referred to her predicament as a "crisis" and a "conflict" as her formerly held beliefs about education were at odds with the position and role she had to assume. Further, her inability to select her classroom placement led to a sense of powerlessness; specifically, she called herself a "cog" in the system. Though Erica possessed strong opinions and a significant amount of background knowledge with regards to school reform and educational change, her depiction of herself as a cog suggests the extent of her feelings of disempowerment within the district.

Other corps members used course assignments as a way to articulate their concerns about working at turn-around schools in the district and expressed particular frustration with the ways in which these schools framed their mission. Melissa, for example, interpreted Excel's objective as "turning chaos into order":

> The purpose of an [Excel] turn-around school is to come in and impose a system of strict order where there is "chaos" and to determine what children need to learn and how they need to learn it by employing formulaic, scripted curricula and assessments. I have heard my administrators say things to this effect: "Our classrooms provide students with the structure they don't have outside of school," and "Our teachers must be over-planned so that there is never a minute of unstructured time in the classroom."

Thus, some corps members questioned the assumptions behind Excel's agenda from the outset and viewed the goal of creating order as pejorative since it implied that communities were broken, disorderly and chaotic prior to their intervention. In a similar account, another Excel teacher related the following regarding how one student interpreted the drastic changes in the school:

> I taught a couple days of eighth-grade Saturday school here at [Excel]. I said to one of the kids on a Saturday, "What do you think about the change in the school? Do you like it?" He said, "Well, last year was like prison and this year is like prison, but it's different. Last year, you thought you were going to get knifed and that's pretty scary, but this year, there are rules and I don't really know why there are rules. It's like you get a demerit if your shirt is not tucked in. . . . I don't really get why, so it's kind of like prison too." This is a kid who comes to school on time and has never had a detention and he goes completely unnoticed in the system because he doesn't act out. He's not a behavior problem. He's reading on grade level. That concerns me. The little ones feel so loved and everything is new, so it's great, but I don't know if we're helping those in-between kids to say, "It's the same to me whether I get knifed or Big Brother is watching me." It was the same to him. It's prison. It's all prison. That scared me a little bit.

Mainstream narratives concerning education reform initiatives often construe change as unequivocally positive. By exploring the perspective of an older student who experienced the turnaround transformation quite differently from either the teachers or younger students who were new to the school, this corps member was unearthing and engaging with the complexities inherent in the school reform process. As the student suggested, the word "prison" indexes not only violence and chaos but also equally disturbing notions of control and obedience.

Conclusion

Corps members arriving in Ridgeville during the 2010–2011 school year entered a highly charged political context characterized by the expansion of charter schools and a shift towards highly scripted curricular programs and rigid instructional mandates. Moreover, the reach and influence of TFA within the Ridgeville district were both expanding, with an increasing number of inexperienced teachers being placed in underserved city schools. Although most corps members entered Ridgeville with little formal education experience or preparation, most approached the institutional contexts critically and engaged directly and purposefully with dominant narratives of school reform, which extolled the virtues of charter schools and limited the efficacy of teachers. Thus, from the beginning corps members were aware of a number of contradictions, namely, their simultaneous positioning as agents of change within a failing district and low-status workers told to follow orders and heed authority at all costs.

Chapter 3

"THE TENSION BETWEEN URGENCY AND HUMANITY": CONFRONTING FACTORY-STYLE EDUCATION

As teachers worked to make sense of the contradictions they encountered in Ridgeville, they began to theorize their experiences using lenses that highlighted their lack of agency and feelings of disempowerment. Specifically, corps members consistently invoked metaphors which likened their experiences as teachers to those of factory workers. These tensions became more complex in light of the identity work that teachers were doing as they sought to adopt and enact identities as teachers. As the various institutional contexts to which the teachers belonged exerted a moralistic and technical control over them and reinforced their status as low-level workers, it became increasingly difficult for the corps members to resist these identity designations or imagine alternate possibilities for themselves and their students.

Becoming Teachers

In his article "Identity as an Analytic Lens for Research in Education," James Gee (2000) posits that one meaning of identity involves being recognized as a certain "kind of person" (p. 99). As new urban schoolteachers, first-year corps members must shun their former identity as students and contend with what it means to be recognized by students, parents, colleagues and district personnel as "teachers." While Gee suggests that we are born into certain identity categories (what he calls Nature identities, or N-identities), other categories are assigned to us by the institutions to which we belong (I-identities).

Because many corps members never planned for a career in education—and were just recently students themselves—taking up the identity of "urban teacher" which institutions like TFA and the school district bestowed upon them is particularly challenging. Further, many corps members joined TFA without having a realistic picture of what taking on the identity of urban teacher might entail. The corps members in this study, for example, were recruited largely from elite colleges and universities from which it was difficult to imagine the challenges of working in impoverished, urban communities. As Cecily explained,

> There are CMs [corps members] coming from different situations, but a large majority of the people are signing on before they've even graduated in their senior year. Things look pretty rosy in the spring your senior year and you feel ready.

Here Cecily acknowledged that recruitment of corps members generally occurred at a time characterized by a unique sense of comfort and optimism—the final semester of college. Alex added to this sentiment by stating that

> I was able to figure out that when you're a college junior and you're applying to TFA and you don't know anything about education because you were not an education major because they don't hire education majors, you have these sort of hunky dory ideas about school and you have these romanticized notions about what your schooling was like. You're like, "Yeah, I can teach. Anybody can do that."

Alex, like Cecily, worried that new corps members entered TFA with romanticized notions of teaching and were subsequently disheartened when the work proved emotionally trying or when the "Institutional identities" to which they were meant to adhere proved too contrastive to their previous identities as high-performing students at elite institutions. Alex went on to state the following:

> I think to throw a recent college grad into a very professionalized and politicized environment that is a public school with the unions and you're now a professional person. You're no longer a student. Just to throw a very immature college student into that environment I think is misguided. Also throwing them into an environment where they're on their own and they're responsible for the education of twenty little souls is again misguided. There is no way you could expect a twenty-one-year-old to do that effectively.

In addition to the jarring reality of leaving behind a student lifestyle, corps members had to confront the ways in which institutions like Teach For America and the Ridgeville School District "authorized" certain identities (Gee, 2000). This sense of "authorization" had significant implications for corps members who struggled to conform to an image of urban teaching which emphasized order, control and a mechanized approach to teaching and learning.

According to Gee (2000), one of the most interesting aspects of Institutional identities is that they "can be put on a continuum in terms of how actively or passively the occupant of a position fills or fulfills his or her role or duties" (p. 103). In other words, sometimes Institutional identities are imposed and thus resisted, while at other times they are embraced. For example, some corps members in this study took issue with the kind of teacher identity they were asked to adopt, while others willingly accepted such identities, in part because images of other, possible ways of being were not always readily available.

In addition to the N-identities and I-identities noted above, Gee also discusses the role of Discourse identities (or D-identities) in further considering the ways in which recognition as a certain kind of person occurs. In theorizing D-identities, Gee discusses their historical and social dimensions of discourse and comments on the notion that a person cannot be recognized in a particular way unless existing discourses allow for this kind of recognition. Teach For America corps members, who are situated within a national context of widespread urban school reform and sweeping educational change, rely on these discourses to inform their understandings of themselves as "reformers" seeking to transform unjust aspects of society. Many corps members, for example, indicated that their decision to pursue urban teaching was connected to a broader historical and political discourse, which depicted education as the Civil Rights issue of the generation. In accordance with this stance, one corps member stated the following:

> Education is the answer to so many things. If people have an education, there are so many more opportunities available. It's the solution to so many things and so many of the ills of poverty and people making foolish decisions and things like that have their roots in education.

Further, according to Gee, institutions can and do draw upon popular discourses in order to instill I-identities. TFA, for example, was able to capitalize upon the corps members' desires to work for educational change as part of their initial recruitment processes. Convinced that addressing educational inequities would promote a broader agenda of justice in U.S. society, Erica noted that

> I came into doing this, you know, I had personal reasons and personal beliefs that were behind it. And I don't know. Maybe it's somewhat idealistic. I thought—like for me if I'm totally honest and real about it education is the silver bullet. That's really what I

believe in. And for me, maybe I won't teach forever and maybe I won't ever be a great teacher, but I think our schools are what have to be changed to make changes for other things that I'm really passionate about. Like I'm really passionate about climate change and I'm really upset about poverty and there are a lot of things I think that education influences.

To Erica, education has the potential to solve a host of societal problems and her decision to enter education as an idealistic college graduate most likely reflected her broader desire to work for good in society and a commensurate conviction that education is the surest medium by which to do so. Interestingly, even early into her first year of teaching, she acknowledged the possibility that she may not stay in the classroom long term. However, her definition of education extends beyond school walls, suggesting that she believes that her work for societal transformation will continue whether or not she remains in a traditional school setting.

Taking on the identity of "urban teacher" was not an easy or fluid process for most corps members, as is demonstrated throughout the remainder of this book. Corps members, at various junctures, accepted and rejected the institutional and discursive identities that attempted to recognize them as certain kinds of people and certain kinds of teachers. As corps members worked to reconcile their expectations for themselves and their students with the limiting portrayals of urban schooling that characterized the discourse of TFA and the district, many came to embody the tension that commonly accompanies difficult questions of identity. Thus, even the most idealistic corps members had trouble subverting the pervasive atmosphere of control long enough to imagine themselves as creative and capable practitioners.

Moralistic and Technical Control

Though teachers like Erica enter the field with a sense of idealism and a strong desire to influence the life chances of their students and contribute meaningfully to the broader school reform agenda, the corps members in my courses continually expressed frustration with what Achinstein and Ogawa (2006) refer to as the moralistic and technical control exerted by Teach For America, the Excel Charter Network and the Ridgeville School District.

According to Achinstein and Ogawa (2006), recent changes in education policy, including the increased emphasis on assessment as well as more prescribed instructional approaches, have led to what they call "a potent control system" (p. 53). Educators within their study used dramatic language to characterize program oversight. For example, one teacher described her district and school as "prison-like" (p. 38). The curriculum consultants who came periodically to monitor whether the program was being implemented "faithfully" were referred to at different times as "Nazis" and "police." Achinstein and Ogawa (2006) use the term technical control to refer to the ways in which school districts exact control by mandating certain curricular and pedagogical approaches. By moralistic control, the authors are invoking a policy environment that demands "compliance with institutional norms and values through ideological means that determine what is and is not allowable in a given system, and thus serves to legitimize the system" (p. 32).

Because the corps members were, for the most part, young and inexperienced, it became easier for the district and the Excel Charter Network to exert both moralistic and technical control. Even from the initial interviews which determined their school placements, corps members struggled to express their misgivings concerning their work environment. Primarily, many teachers do not see themselves as knowledgeable enough about the field of education to assert beliefs or make decisions that run counter to the culture of their schools or Teach For America, a phenomenon that is explored more extensively in Chapter 5. Second, if corps members did choose to outwardly oppose particular mandates, they would risk isolation and quite possibly censure from both peers and administrators, Katrina, a second-year corps member, detailed her conflict over whether to heed curricular mandates. Like many corps members she had to reconcile her desire to keep her job and continue her work with students with the conviction that certain district mandates were harming the very children she sought to help:

> I've had a very difficult year where I went into the year like, "Screw everyone. I'm doing it. I don't care if they fire me," to then very quickly seeing the climate of my school and the incredible shift in the principal and realizing that I couldn't have that attitude or I really was going to be fired. That was really rough. For a while, I just went with the script because I had to, and that was when I wanted to quit. I just realized I would rather be fired than keep doing this stuff that is harming my kids.

In addition to the moralistic pressure to conform to certain instructional approaches, many teachers experience the technical control exerted by the district as a means of surveillance. In order to theorize the ways in which societies attempt to control their members, Foucault (1977) used the revolutionary 18th-century prison design of the "Panopticon" as a societal metaphor. Designed by Jeremy Bentham, the Panopticon places prisoners under constant observation, unable either to escape from or to return the gaze of authorities. According to Foucault (1977), "the major effect of the Panopticon [is]: to induce in the inmate a state of conscious and permanent visibility that assures the automatic functioning of power" (p. 201). Within the Panopticon, power was constantly visible but remained unverifiable. In other words, inmates were always in sight of the tower from which they were presumably observed yet could not discern whether anyone was in the tower at a given moment. Individuals subject to such observation, according to Bentham, will eventually internalize the gaze and monitor their own behavior. Self-discipline will replace coercion as the method of social control. Ultimately, then, "a real subjection is born mechanically from a fictitious relation" (Foucault, 1977, p. 202). Invoking the effects of this kind of surveillance, teachers used class discussions as a way to process the overpowering sense of fear related to the constant observation exercised by school and district personnel. One corps member, in particular, shared that the constant threat of surveillance decreased her motivation and compromised her approaches so that she was not able to do what she considered to be in the best interest of her students:

> I'm having a hard time even motivating myself. I'm so afraid someone is going to walk into the room and see me doing something I'm not supposed to be doing even though it's "what I think is best for the kids," so I'm not motivated to even go there because I'm a first-year teacher. I don't want to get into trouble. Maybe that makes me like a follow-the-rules kind of girl but it's just killing my motivation essentially and that's really bothering me.

In a similar account, Christa noted the overwhelming sense of fear that impeded her desire to experiment with either her curriculum or instructional approach:

> Due to my inexperience with the teaching profession and the fact that we are pressured to do so by the administration, I am one of the teachers that follows the teaching manual religiously. Perhaps as a crutch, but perhaps out of fear of administrative retribution. I rely heavily on the teacher's manual to conduct my literacy lessons. My students' needs, not the curriculum, should drive the literacy instruction, but this is not the case in my classroom. If we have strayed even a hair from the curriculum when someone from the administrative leadership team walks into the classroom, the children will be barked at, any shred of classroom management will be completely usurped.

Christa's use of language in this instance suggests the kind of toll that surveillance can exact on teachers. For example, she noted that she must follow the teaching manual "religiously" in fear of "retribution" from her administration. Further, she contended that any deviation from the script could result in her classroom being usurped by angry administrators. Although she acknowledged that her students' needs were not being met, the threat of administrative surveillance kept her from experimenting with her instruction. This form of control began to infiltrate the consciousness of the teachers, as they were never sure when they would be subject to observation and evaluation. Thus, like Foucault's prisoners, they soon began to monitor themselves. Teachers also started to doubt their own sense of efficacy in the classroom and adopt a more passive orientation towards teaching and learning as a way to compensate for these kinds of control mechanisms. For example, one corps member stated the following:

> I don't know what my objective is at the end of the year because I'm not put in a situation where I need to research that for myself. It's like this self-fulfilling prophecy of teachers that don't work hard or care about their job, so just what people try to say about teachers all the time, but you create a situation in which you have a curriculum and pacing guides where everything is done for you. It's begging for you not to work. You're going against the grain by trying to work hard on your curriculum. Spending time on it means you're probably not being faithful. It's kind of insane.

Although TFA teachers are commonly recruited for their diligence and intelligence, these traits were not rewarded in Ridgeville. The TFA website, for example, asserts that critical thinking skills, perseverance in the face of challenges and demonstrated leadership capabilities are the characteristics that are most valued in potential corps members (www.teachforamerica.org). Despite these claims, many corps members find that a premium is placed on following orders, obeying rules and trusting a curriculum that they find problematic and fallible. Thus, the corps members' predicament closely mirrors that of their students who, subject to a "no-excuses" approach to teaching and learning, must conform to a militaristic environment that seeks to regulate and control every aspect of their educational experience (Lack, 2009). For example, one corps member described an experience she had during an Excel-sponsored professional development session as an exercise in conformity and compliance:

> I think it's also who has trained us like, "Sit down, dummy. Watch the blue screen, the white screen with the little blue and red writing on the bottom. Follow along with the script. Write down the notes and keep it moving." It's not really a cognitive experience. It's like the same as what we are teaching our kids: "Follow what I say. I snap, you

speak. Answer that question." You're told what to think. . . . There is only one way to teach, one way to learn and one way to behave.

These modes of surveillance are not unlike Gramsci's notions of hegemony in which control is not maintained through the use of violence or economic coercion but through the use of "common sense" or popular ideology (as cited in Kenway, 2001). According to Gramsci, the "naturalization" of certain ideas and ideologies is ultimately what makes them effective as controlling mechanisms. As new teachers are socialized to accept the dominant school reform narrative of "back to basics" and tightly controlled behavior management as the primary remedies for improving urban schools, the proliferation of other, alternative narratives are effectively squelched. For example, Ridgeville corps members placed within the Excel Charter Network had to contend with narratives concerning the best approach for helping remedial readers. In an attempt to emphasize phonics and basic reading skills, the Excel Charter Network selected a curriculum called "Reading Mastery" as one of the primary pillars of its early childhood literacy program. Though corps members expressed doubts over its integrity, they were told repeatedly not to raise these questions but rather to follow orders:

> Honestly, the ways I teach literacy, to me, feels very, very disjointed and one is the scripted curriculum, which doesn't seem to have a lot of coherence but it's very minutely spiraled all the way through and the teachers are told, "Don't question it. It works."

Once again, corps members were told they must blindly follow a set curriculum and remain silent despite their doubts or misgivings. As one corps member noted in a discussion:

> One of the teachers at our school who has been teaching for seven years and, to my understanding, has been teaching "Reading Mastery" every single year at all levels from kindergarten through fifth grade, she says, "Don't worry about it. It works. I promise. Just teach it." That's not enough of an answer to me.

The corps members found themselves in settings in which learning to teach was translated into following rules. As the corps members, despite their objections, began to internalize these curricular and pedagogical mandates, they exerted the same control over their students which they themselves had experienced at the hands of their respective schools and the district at large:

In terms of teaching philosophy, I think my ideas are very much based around wanting kids to feel like they have agency in their own learning. I want them to feel like they're agents that have power, that they're agents who make decisions and they are choosing different activities and that they learn in the way that fits them and learn to pursue their interests. However, the message I send out every day to my kids is, "Sit down and listen to me. I am the holder of this knowledge. If you sit down, listen, fold your hands and sit up straight up and sit like a star, then you'll go to college and be successful." That's the message.

This corps member, for example, was aware of the dissonance that existed between her desire to impart agency to her students and the pedagogical reality she enacted on a daily basis. Similarly, another corps member shared how the evaluative framework imposed by the school undermined her desire to get to know her students and to use that knowledge as a means for effective teaching:

But at the same time I'm just beginning to scratch the surface of them as people, but I've known them for three months, and I'm realizing how little I actually know about them. And how little I actually have access to why they do this, and what is the root of this behavior, and why do they struggle with this so much. And there aren't any formulas for stuff like that. . . . I end up worrying a lot more about what people are going to say when they evaluate me rather than being in the moment and taking advantage of that moment and these minutes that I have with the kids.

This corps member aptly recognized the limitations inherent in the teaching approach she was required to use and struggled to reconcile the need to be present with students and the stress and concern which accompany frequent evaluation. Oakes, Franke, Quartz, and Rogers (2002) echo these teachers' concerns when they assert that urban teachers "need to understand local urban cultures, the urban political economy, the bureaucratic structure of urban schools, and the community and social service support networks serving urban centers" (p. 228). While corps members undoubtedly recognize the importance of getting to know both their students and the local context, bureaucratic obstacles often make these encounters impossible. Many corps members also worried that in addition to not having the institutional support to invest in their students as people, the kinds of values imparted by Excel and the school district limited the possibilities of "success" available to the children they taught. For example, Dierdre noted that because of the disproportionate emphasis on obedience and order within Excel, quiet students tended to be more successful:

Literally on Friday, I heard a teacher say, "Oh, he's a great kid. He doesn't say much. He's a great student. He's really quiet." Excel's ideal student is someone who is docile, someone who follows directions, someone who sits up straight, folds their hands, tracks the speaker and will never challenge you. Nothing. That's the ideal student. That's what we are pushing our students towards. The kids who don't fit that are ostracized.

Drawing a connection between the labor force and public school students, Ira Shor (1980) writes, "At the very least, supervisors discourage people talking to each other because it interferes with productivity in school, teachers dissuade students from talking to each other, or out of turn, not only to maintain order but also to maintain the teacher as sole regulator of talking" (p. 72). Dierdre, like many corps members in Ridgeville, was concerned about the depictions of students and teachers suggested by local reform initiatives. As a result, she actively sought to use course discussions, assignments and other collaborative settings to challenge and complicate her experiences with the curricular and instructional mandates levied by both Excel and the school district.

The Paradox of Taylorism and Innovation

When asked in an interview about his experiences teaching within the school district, Alex, a second-year corps member, used the word "Taylorism" to describe his tenure:

> I am not going to articulate this very well, but there is sort of a move towards corpora-tizing schools and making schools like little companies and superintendents and CEOs and they issue mandates that get pushed down. It's almost like Taylorism, especially with direct instruction, every single minute of the day is planned. You're a little robot up there reading from the script. There are some very corporate models. If we just put a lot of money in schools, we will fix them and we get lots of CEOs opening charter schools or whatever donating money not knowing what the hell they're doing quite frankly. I think that TFA really subscribes to that sort of corporate model where there's a student and the student is a vessel. You have knowledge and you have 180 school days to cram that little head with knowledge, because if you don't, they're going to fall behind and they're never going to catch up to their more affluent peers. It's a race, it's a race, it's a race.

His invocation of Taylorism and its application to education invited me to think differently regarding the ways in which corps members were describing their experiences with local and national reform efforts. In reviewing the data during the analysis process, I discovered that references to Taylorism were peppered throughout the written and oral discourse of the corps members in my class. Moreover, I began to view Taylorism as a useful lens for understanding the dehumanizing dimensions of reform initiatives.

Taylorism has a long history within the realm of public education and stems from the work of Frederick Taylor, who coined the term "scientific management" as he attempted to find ways to increase efficiency and maximize industrial output at the turn of the 20th century (Callahan, 1962). Although his work was originally intended for use by railroads, Taylor's ideas were soon applied to all sectors of society, including public education. Because Taylor's primary concerns involved increasing efficiency and minimizing waste, he asserted that systematic, scientific study would reveal the singularly best method for accomplishing a particular task. Once this method was determined, the responsibilities of the worker greatly diminished and she/he only had to follow a prescribed set of orders. In other words, "In [Taylor's] system the judgment of the individual workman was replaced by the laws, rules, principles, etc., of the job which was developed by management" (Callahan, 1962, p. 28).

Although Callahan's critique of the application of Taylorism to public schooling was written in 1962, it continues to have relevance today as teachers contend with what Au (2011) refers to as the "New Taylorism." Au argues that the work of public school teachers is controlled by high-stakes testing and prescriptive curricular programs, a notion which resonates with the ways in which Ridgeville corps members described their socialization and training. According to Noble, for Taylor, "efficient production relied upon the factory managers' ability to gather all the information possible about the work which they oversaw, systematically analyze it according to 'scientific' methods, figure out the most efficient ways for workers to complete individual tasks, and then tell the worker exactly how to produce their products in an ordered manner" (as cited in Au, 2011). Similarly, the classrooms in which many of the corps members worked were tightly controlled environments in which teachers had to meticulously track student achievement, monitor behavior through the use of incentives and follow a routinized lesson format which included direct instruction, guided practice and independent practice.

Alex's concerns, noted above, about the influence of corporations over the practices of public and charter schools were not unfounded. Au (2011) argued that under No Child Left Behind (NCLB) "teachers in many low performing US districts have been required to use commercially packaged reading instruction programs such as Open Court, which tell teachers exactly what page to be on for each day as well as every word and line they are allowed to say while teaching reading, all in preparation for the high-stakes testing" (p. 32). Wendy, a first-year corps member, reflected on the personal toll exacted by having to implement this kind of prescribed academic program:

I am a piece of a larger systemic process that forces an undifferentiated and hardly rigorous curriculum on my students. It is indeed a literacy and math plan that does not value my students as individuals. I am a tool in executing this. It is an example of systemic inequality that gets perpetuated every day within my classroom, my school and "urban" and under-resourced schools across the country.

Although Wendy was teaching within a particular, localized context, she was aware that her situation reflected larger systemic trends throughout the country and worried about her role in this broader, oppressive system.

The Excel Charter Network further reinforced these aspects of Taylorism within schools through its strict control of pedagogical approaches. For example, one slide in a PowerPoint presentation given by the leadership from Excel during the fall of 2010 depicted a large red X over the following words: project-based, inquiry-based, text-based and student-interest-based, indicating that these modes of learning should not be implemented within Excel's network of schools. The facilitator went on to mention that it was simply more efficient to tell students what they needed to know (personal notes, October 20, 2010). It is evident that Excel's hope in emphasizing efficiency at the expense of experimentation and exploration is for "breakthrough academic success" (Excel Instructional Guidebook). The model that Excel promotes may indeed help students achieve at greater levels on standardized measures; yet, as Kliebard (1975) notes, "As in industry, the price of worship at the altar of efficiency is the alienation of the worker from his work—where continuity and wholeness of the enterprise are destroyed for those who engage in it" (as cited in Au, 2011, p. 1). Thus, the tension surrounding an emphasis on efficiency invites deeper questions regarding the overall purposes of school reform and the meaning of education.

Although control and efficiency are lauded within the classroom by both Teach For America and the Excel Charter Network, TFA does encourage innovation once teachers have left the classroom. Moreover, this entrepreneurship is supported through a variety of institutional mechanisms which provide teachers with funding and support to create new organizations, design educational alternatives and experiment with teaching and learning. For example, Denis, a second-year corps member, planned to start a summer literacy organization once he'd finished his two-year commitment with TFA, an initiative that was encouraged by TFA in a number of ways:

I think it [TFA] also encourages people to be entrepreneurial and it gives you this avenue to do it. Also there's a lot of support. . . . I have a bunch of thought partners and people who are advisors to the project. There is a woman in TFA who runs the social entrepreneurship program there. Whenever I have an application I send, we go back and forth on it a lot. As part of the TFA prize for winning the thing, there are two consultants who are entrepreneurs themselves. They started a venture capital by funding and also consulting for young education organizations, so they pick a small number of organizations and try to help them gestate into something bigger. They have been consulting for free on my project, which is super helpful. They know stuff that I don't know. They were at TFA and they were in finance for five years. Now they're going back to this, so they have that experience that I don't at all have, or I have had for a month or whatever, and it's super helpful.

Denis used this support to his advantage and through it was able to lay the foundation to begin his summer literacy work. He acknowledged, however, that the energy he devoted to his literacy start-up exacted a toll on his classroom teaching:

> I feel bad about the fact that a lot of my energy has been put into the start-up, so much so that I feel like I've put my classroom in cruise control more than I would have liked to. At the beginning of the year, I was really excited about how the classroom was. Now I still am, but I feel like when I go home, my mind is immediately in start-up mode and thirty minutes before I go to bed, I'll bang out a lesson plan. I feel like I enjoy my time at school but I feel like too much of my energy is somewhere else for it to get to the next level of teaching, you know what I mean?

What is most troubling about Denis's account is the fact that the attention he devoted to his start-up organization significantly detracted from his classroom practice, an ideological shift that was encouraged by TFA through the kinds of support present for innovation and entrepreneurship. He noted that he was not able to reach "the next level" with regards to teaching because his energy was diverted to his start-up efforts. Interestingly, the entrepreneurial supports offered to corps members are, in some ways, more robust than those designed to support them as classroom teachers.

These institutional emphases send a distinct message—the classroom is the space in which one follows orders, while innovation will occur elsewhere. Numerous corps members, for example, shared disdain for their summer preparation conducted during the TFA Institute, believing that teaching was reduced to a formulaic prescription and its complexities and nuances elided. With only five weeks allotted for formal training during the summer before they were to begin teaching full-time, many corps members felt that TFA focused on the most efficient means of "training" possible. As one corps member shared:

And I felt like that's how all of institute was—this is the most executable way to teach a bunch of non-experienced people how to be a teacher in five weeks and you can take this and you can do it and maybe it's not the most thought-provoking and maybe it's not the most successful way to teach but it's the most efficient for the amount of time we have and now off you go. And when you're working with a corps of teachers that you're really expecting to be there for two years, you don't have to be thinking about "these need to be a corps of very reflective people" because they're going to leave before they could ever reach that level of effectiveness as a teacher. So it's such a structure of efficiency and really thinking that the only capital is that they're a body in a room. And if you just follow what we tell you to do, you can't mess it up.

Because corps members were not expected to make a career out of teaching, many believed that they were taught to approach teaching mechanistically and required to follow a set of prescribed steps to reduce the possibility of failure. Teaching was consistently portrayed as a low-skilled occupation that required little creativity, imagination or critical thinking. As Au (2011) notes:

> The metaphor of Taylorism can be mapped on to US schools in a very simple and neat way. Students are the "raw materials" to be produced like commodities according to specified standards and objectives. Teachers are the workers who employ the most efficient methods to get students to meet the pre-determined standards and objectives. Administrators are the managers who determine and dictate to teachers the most efficient methods in the production process. The school is the factory assembly line where this process takes place. (p. 27)

According to this model, teachers have little control over the materials and methods that they use, relying instead on outsiders to guide their choices and decisions, an approach to instruction which ultimately has a dehumanizing effect on both teachers and students. Because of the relentless focus on efficiency and production, teachers began to describe their classroom in ways that echoed the "New Taylorism":

> I think of routines in my own classroom as ways that we cut down on time, very quick things that we do every day, most of it I direct, they [the students] do it and they are praised for doing it quickly and silently. . . . I am placed in a charter system that emphasizes rote recall, traditional bookwork and high levels of student compliance. Because we are a "turnaround school" and working with students who are significantly behind academically there is a culture of "no time to waste" and a strong emphasis on test prep, even in the younger grades.

Similarly, another corps member described how the quest for efficiency manifested itself in her classroom, noting, in particular, the ways in which the abbreviated segments of time limit the possibilities for deep engagement and learning:

> And it needs to be simple and it needs to be quick because they need to be able to do this independent practice in the block of fifteen minutes you have after going through direct instruction, guided practice, and so it never delves deep. It never delves into kids internalizing something and kids really working to generate something. Everything is divided into fifteen minutes and in that block of fifteen minutes, you have to have direct instruction, guided practice, private practice, exit slip.

This piecemeal approach to learning reflects the assembly-line mentality of the factory—as tasks are divided into smaller and smaller pieces, they become increasingly devoid of meaning, leading to an overall sense of dehumanization and isolation both for the student and the teacher.

Urgency and Humanity

As a result, several corps members cited a human cost to the drive for high test scores and academic achievement. Realizing how few opportunities students had in the school day to explore interesting questions, communicate openly in discussion or share personal information led Dierdre, a first-year corps member, to frame the encroachment of Taylorism into public education as a tension between "urgency and humanity." At Excel, in particular, the focus on efficiency is explicitly driven by a sense of urgency, as noted here in the instructional guidebook:

> Urgency must be built and maintained: teachers must keep a laser-beam focus on the lesson objective, ensure student clarity around the purpose of lesson portion, and provide explicit reminders of the need to be urgent.

Dierdre, like other corps members and Excel teachers who were under extreme pressure to raise test scores, struggled with this tension. In particular, Dierdre worried about the human cost of an efficiency-driven model:

> They [the students] clearly perceive the sense of urgency that drives our reading instruction, but I have feared that this urgency was taking away the humanity behind the experience of literature.

A number of corps members echoed Dierdre's concerns, believing that the overemphasis on efficiency had created a dehumanizing classroom environment in which students and teachers were objectified or, as Joey notes below, treated like "cogs in the machine":

> I find this to be particularly true with the amount of urgency that is created in our classrooms. Teachers are pressed to get students to pass exams and meet benchmark results and, in turn, students feel pressured to do well and are merely cogs in the machine.

The limitations of the prescribed curriculum in reflecting the lived experiences of students was mentioned most frequently by African American and Latino corps members who repeatedly commented on the ways in which their cultural histories were marginalized throughout their own K–12 education. Driven by a desire to make their teaching and lessons culturally relevant, many of these teachers were similarly confounded by the limitations of prescribed curricula. For example, even with rich autobiographical histories to draw upon, these teachers found themselves torn between their personal belief that culturally relevant teaching could transform the educational experiences of minority youth and the pressures exerted by their schools to conform to a more mechanistic instructional approach. Dawn, for example, shared the following anecdote in a written assignment:

> When I joined the ranks of Teach For America, it was my honest intention to engage my students in manners that would truly invite them into the classroom. However as a first-year teacher I have found it grueling to do so. . . . However as I consider my students, I see similar sentiments of frustration with schooling that does not include their experience. Their experience mirrors many of the sentiments of disengagement and disenchantment with an educational system that alienates a minority existence that I felt in my own educational experience.

Although Dawn entered Teach For America with the intention of incorporating her students' cultural experiences into her lessons, she ultimately found it "grueling to do so." Similarly, Jayna expressed frustration regarding the ways in which the social studies curriculum explicitly favored European American ideals at the expense of other perspectives. Despite her strong convictions about the inclusion of minority experiences in the classroom, she remained unsure of how to navigate the rigid curriculum to which her school subscribed:

> We live in a society where European American ideals are forced upon the students in our educational system. Despite the fact that America is a melting pot of many different ethnicities, curriculum fails to incorporate other cultures. This is something that I could attest to growing up. For example, we learned on the European American version

of slavery; as though no African American left any information about what they experienced during slavery. . . . I always thought I would introduce my students to various cultures when I taught and now as a teacher, I often wonder how I can incorporate culture into my lessons when I have such a rigid curriculum to follow. Students' various cultures are silenced through the curriculum I have to follow and it is important to their educational success that I allow them to explore and express these cultures.

To some degree these teachers are wrestling with whether their own ideals or desires are compatible within their respective environments, given the constraints. While Jayna and Dawn might have originally imagined themselves as multicultural educators determined to provide an educational experience that addresses the unique needs of their students, they found themselves, instead, confronted by a different reality, one in which they were forced to adhere to pedagogical and curricular approaches which seldom spoke to the unique and differentiated experiences of their students.

Conclusion

The Ridgeville corps members entered a challenging and complex political context with the added burden of having to interpret, adopt and enact the identity of urban educator. While many viewed teaching as the primary avenue for addressing a range of pressing societal concerns, a conviction which helped them to endure trying circumstances, these teachers found themselves subject to systems which framed them as low-level workers and which consistently extolled efficiency at the expense of humanity. Sadly, these conceptions of teaching and teachers began to infiltrate the consciousness of even the most determined corps members, leading to a sense of powerlessness in the face of unyielding curricular mandates. For example, even those teachers who brought their own autobiographical narratives to bear on teaching and learning and expressed a commensurate desire to incorporate a vast spectrum of cultural experiences into their classrooms struggled to make their visions a reality.

However, this chapter primarily aims to illustrate that the lenses which corps members apply to their teaching practice offer valuable insights into how those corps members experienced their socialization as urban educators. The fact that a significant number of corps members drew upon Taylorism and factory metaphors to theorize their experiences within Ridgeville suggests the extent of their disillusionment and disempowerment. Without opportunities to reconcile their hopes for their students with the pressures to conform to a scripted curriculum, the constant threat of administrative surveillance and the emphasis on urgency and efficiency, corps members are more likely to feel overwhelmed and hopeless in their respective settings. By attending to the analytical frames and lenses which they use to make sense of their practice, teacher educators can help corps members reflect upon the very real limitations manifest in their situations and invite corps members to adopt alternate lenses and frameworks which may help them view urban education from a platform of possibility.

Chapter 4
"INFINITE JURISDICTION": MANAGING STUDENT ACHIEVEMENT IN AND OUT OF SCHOOL

Like international humanitarian workers, the Ridgeville corps members were driven by a dual sense of optimism and ambition, eager to remedy societal inequities and willing to relocate to unfamiliar geographic settings in order to do so. Moreover, the corps members I taught seemed to struggle with many of the same broader questions faced by humanitarian workers who choose to go abroad: What is the individual's role in working for large-scale change? Who are the recipients of our help and who is to blame for their problems? What future do we as "helpers" imagine for those we are aiming to help and what actions do we take to achieve these outcomes? What does it mean to leave "the field," and how is the decision to leave justified when the work is clearly unfinished and ongoing?

Like humanitarian workers who must negotiate various bureaucracies to fulfill their mandate to provide assistance to impoverished populations, corps members had to contend with similar complexities in their effort to address the longstanding achievement gap between white and minority students. Moreover, corps members also had specific notions regarding whom they were trying to "help." If critical interventions in any context assume that the "victims" are somehow deficient or lacking in agency, profound change is unlikely. The ways in which corps members both thought about and portrayed their students had significant implications for the ways in which they taught them. Parallels with the field of humanitarian assistance further illustrate how efforts to assist others can be undermined by attempts to control the outcome—an important reminder that "helpers" in any sector of society must constantly reflect upon their motivations and intentions in order to resist colonialist tendencies.

Individual/System

One of the questions that pervaded the discourse of the Ridgeville corps members and proved analogous in many ways to the kinds of issues faced by humanitarian workers was whether deeply rooted societal problems like poverty could be remedied through individual effort. For the TFA corps members this question manifested itself with regards to the achievement gap and whether the persistent, "relentless" work of a single teacher could affect such a seemingly intractable issue. In her examination of John Ogbu's landmark work on minority youth in Shaker Heights, Ohio, Gibson (2005) considers the broad range of factors that contribute to minority student achievement including relationships with teachers and peers, community forces and home/school connections. Thus while Gibson contends that student/teacher relationships are critical to academic achievement, the broad range of factors she highlights suggests that only wider systemic change can truly transform student achievement. For the past two decades, TFA has attempted to close the achievement gap between white and minority students through the efforts of its educators, yet little concrete evidence exists to demonstrate that these efforts have been successful on a broader scale. Similarly, despite significant increases in foreign aid over the past fifty years and a more pervasive presence of humanitarian workers abroad, some scholars argue that the problems of the world's poor have persisted and in some cases worsened since the advent of large-scale humanitarian assistance (Anderson, 1998; Easterly, 2006). David Kennedy (2004), for example, notes that "human rights remedies, even when successful, treat the symptoms rather than the illness and this allows the illness not only to fester but to seem like health itself. . . . Even where victims are recompensed or violations avoided, the distributions of power and wealth which produced the violation may well come to seem more legitimate as they seek other avenues of expression" (as cited in Dawes, 2007, p. 15). By using the word "illness" one might assume that Kennedy is referencing the systemic, global forces that conspire to keep people alienated, victimized and impoverished. Similarly, within the realm of urban education, standardized test scores begin to function as artificial indices for determining the relative success or failure of a particular educational intervention, allowing systemic issues to be ignored in favor of the achievements or failures of individual students, teachers, principals or schools. While individual corps members may indeed help students achieve at increased levels on standardized measures, TFA, as an entity, has shown only mixed results in its efforts to improve educational outcomes writ large—an issue which invites scrutiny into what other interventions might inspire more lasting, widespread change (Boyd, Grossman, Lankford, Loeb, & Wyckoff, 2006; Darling-Hammond, Holtzman, Gatlin, & Heilig, 2005; Decker, Mayer, & Glazerman, 2004; Laczko-Kerr & Berliner, 2002).

Tension surrounding the achievement gap and the efficacy of the individual was pervasive during the academic year in which this study took place due to the outcomes of a series of surveys administered by TFA. According to some corps members, surveys conducted by TFA intending to gauge teacher satisfaction and efficacy indicated that the Ridgeville corps members reported less satisfaction and a lower sense of agency than those TFA teachers serving in other regions. The most controversial question on the survey, however, concerned whether corps members believed they could personally contribute to the elimination of the achievement gap. Though deeply committed to their work to address educational injustice, many corps members were unsure of their individual capacity to work towards closing the achievement gap. In describing these kinds of survey questions, one corps member noted the tension surrounding beliefs about student achievement:

> We have a lot of surveys we take throughout the year, but I guess what I've heard anecdotally is that they always ask us this question: Has our two-year experience contributed to our belief that the achievement gap can be closed? And we have the lowest rates of agreement with that statement. . . . But that's not what TFA wants for its mission. They want people to come out like, "Yes, we can do it. It's easy and it's fixed."

Although corps members signed on to TFA knowing that the organization's mission was aimed explicitly at eliminating the achievement gap, many of the corps members interpreted TFA's expectations of them as unreasonable, noting that the possibility of closing the achievement gap—even in one elementary school classroom—in two years' time was impossible. Moreover, some interpreted the mission as a sense of duty or personal responsibility, thus placing a tremendous burden on themselves.

As a result of TFA's emphasis on measurable outcomes, a number of corps members reported feeling that the very qualities that made them compelling TFA recruits—for example, a strong desire to work for social justice or a penchant for innovation and inquiry—were summarily dismissed in favor of a demonstrated ability to raise test scores, which is TFA's primary gauge for progress. One corps member, for example, shared the following during a focus group:

TFA recruits people that have all of these ideals about how education and social justice, all of these fantastic, progressive ideas that definitely the three of us share. . . . And TFA recruits you because of those things, then you get into TFA and they are like, "Oh, all of that stuff we wanted you for? That's all gone. You've got to get the data and you're not a leader unless you're going to do that."

Further, according to these corps members, individuals who did elicit the desired test results from students were lauded as exemplary educators, an accolade which isolated other corps members and diminished a sense of teamwork and collaboration early on:

So some of the recruits are exactly what they want and they make such heroes out of those people that you feel this big. You know what I mean? I feel like this summer there were very specific individuals who were constantly made to be the gods and goddesses of Institute. . . . Remember that guy from Baltimore? He was everywhere. He was like a poster child. It's based on some criteria that is [sic] so in conflict with the reason that they picked me. He did exactly how you told him to so he's a fit. He did everything you told him to and got the results and now he's the best. You do it exactly how they told you to but you don't get that. It's like, "Oh, you're not doing it right."

Believing they were recruited for certain individual characteristics that set them apart, corps members expressed confusion when told to conform to one particular model for teaching or when one measure of success—the test score— was granted sole legitimacy as evidence of achievement. Further, even when corps members tried to forgo their individual beliefs and talents and conform to the expectations outlined by TFA, they often were still unable to produce the kinds of results that TFA expected. Although corps members readily acknowledge the problematic aspects of testing—namely, the ways in which it limits critical thinking and the fact that numbers can be arbitrary markers of success or failure—they are still judged and therefore controlled by these measures. Popkewitz (1998) similarly notes that the true "power" of testing lies in "its disciplining effect" (p. 109). Testing, in other words, can limit and inscribe the identities of both students and teachers. In a sense, the test score becomes fetishized as the key indicator of progress. Corps members are judged externally on whether their students have achieved 80% mastery on a given task. As Popkewitz (1998) states, "Testing programs serve as an important horizon by which corps members judge their teaching practices and students' thinking" (p. 111).

In addition to their frustration regarding the overemphasis on testing data, corps members also expressed concerns over whether the achievement gap could be eliminated given the current social, political and economic climate of the United States. As Alex stated,

> It would be nice to say, "Yes, the achievement gap will close one day." But it's been there for the entire history of mankind. There's always been an underclass. Yes, there is social mobility and the underclass of one generation can move into the middle class in another generation so that can certainly happen, but there is always an underclass.

Alex, like many of the corps members, was actively wrestling with the complexity of social mobility and whether current economic and political conditions actually allow for mass movement into a middle-class position. Similarly, Nicolas retained awareness that his work, however important, was nested within larger systems that undoubtedly affect the life chances and future outcomes for his students:

> Circumstances create neighborhoods, not vice versa. If there were better education, more jobs and the like, fewer people would go to jail. That is a crucial point forgotten by many.

Alex's and Nicolas's questions and concerns serve as evidence that TFA corps members, like all new teachers who choose to enter low-income settings, must contend with racial and economic inequality and its relationship to academic achievement. Corps members consistently expressed their need for forums in which to explicitly discuss how macro-scale societal issues influenced the daily work of teaching and learning. Further, corps members might feel more comfortable addressing issues related to racism or poverty that arise in their classroom if they had the support of a consistent professional community. For example, Achinstein and Ogawa (2006) remind us that individuals working alone are seldom effective in bringing about large-scale change: "there are limits to individual resistance which leave the individual vulnerable and can even result in reproducing the status quo" (p. 57). The authors further contend, through the contrasting portraits of two teachers, that professional communities and collaborative spaces are critical to the intellectual and emotional growth of new teachers. Similarly, Oakes, Franke, Quartz & Rogers (2002) assert that "once students enter a teacher education program, they need to become members of stable learning communities where they reflect together on the intersection of research and theory with teaching practices in urban schools" (p. 231). In studying their own urban teacher preparation program, Oakes et al.

(2002) found that community belonging was an essential factor in young teachers' decision to remain in urban classrooms.

With community at the foreground of my planning process, I sought to design a course which continually emphasized the practice of shared inquiry. From the start of the semester, corps members were placed in inquiry groups of three or four students. I designed these groups with a number of factors in mind including grade level, gender, cultural/racial background, personality and perspectives on teaching. Students met in their groups each week, though the types of interactions varied in accordance with the topic discussed. During some class sessions, corps members were asked to share their written assignments with their group members. At other times, they were asked to analyze and perform a piece of children's literature. Most often, they met to collaborate on designing and planning an interdisciplinary unit which they would teach towards the end of the course. As the course progressed, corps members seemed to become more comfortable with sharing their work publicly and collaborating to produce lesson plans and assignments. As complicated and difficult subjects emerged, for example, immigration reform, welfare and home literacy practices, the inquiry groups became a space in which students could explore their stance on a particular topic before presenting it to the whole group. Although I often assigned specific topics or activities, inquiry groups most often ended up discussing their students and their families, revealing rich and complex narratives regarding what it means to be an outsider in a particular community with the goal of "helping others."

Narratives of Students and Families

Equally consequential to the endeavors of the corps members in my courses was a conception of whom they were hoping to "help" in the Ridgeville communities they entered. Like international aid work in which the work is done to rather than with the local constituents (Anderson, 1998), urban students and families are often rendered silent by the systems designed to support them. According to Anderson (1998), international aid focuses almost entirely on the "concentration of delivery of things to these people, rather than on problem-solving with them and thus places the beneficiaries of aid in a passive, accepting role" (p. 140). This phenomenon can be understood, at least in part, by the ways in which teachers discursively construct their students. These depictions were most prominent in the classroom vignettes which corps members composed and shared publicly as a course assignment at the beginning of the semester. Although the parameters of the assignment were intentionally vague—they were asked only to describe a critical incident from their teaching—most chose to write about their shock at discovering students' academic deficits. Siena wrote about how one of her early literacy lessons failed when she inadvertently embarrassed a fourth-grade student who had not learned to read:

> Now I am standing over his desk with the teacher look I have learned to own. I address the rest of the students, telling them to put their hands down because Thomas is going to read. I bend down, point to where he should be and when he looks up from *Shiloh* his face is red and tears are streaming from his face. At that moment, I realize that Thomas hasn't learned how to read, and that while I thought I was teaching him a lesson on paying attention, he felt embarrassed and attacked.

Dawn, in a separate vignette, outlined a similar account:

> Once I conferred with Kyear, I noticed Curtis who had a book open, but whose eyes couldn't have been further away from the text. As I approached Curtis, I asked him questions about the book, of the same vein as those I asked Kyear. However, this time, my questions were only answered by blank stares. I decided to try a new approach and asked Curtis to read the story from the beginning aloud. Curtis began to smile and "read" a logically founded story; however, none of the words were from the page in front of him. It quickly became evident that Curtis did not know how to read.

Numerous corps members used the vignettes as a means to contend with and theorize student underachievement. In recounting these incidents, teachers expressed their frustration quite honestly. In response to a student repeatedly seeking support, for example, Nicolas wrote, "These kids, I mutter to myself. No work ethic, no focus, no effort. I have a lot of work to do this year." Similarly, Melinda was struck by one first-grader's "lackluster performance" on a sight word challenge activity, writing, "I wondered how she was able to pass so long without her teachers or parents noticing her ignorance." Another teacher lamented that working with her students on a reading activity taught her the true meaning of the word "behind."

As the course progressed and more invitations were offered to consider student achievement from a range of different perspectives, an increasing number of corps members began to reflect critically upon the ways in which their beliefs about students' capabilities would come to affect not only their teaching but also their broader hopes for educational equity. For example, when offered the opportunity to reflect on her vignette about a student's struggle to spell "basic" words, Dierdre immediately recognized and problematized her use of deficit language by writing, "Rather than phrasing this as a deficit, what are different ways I can utilize what V. already has, focusing on buttressing those skills with reading and writing fluency he needs in the classroom?" Joey, when given the opportunity to re-write his vignette, noted the narrow definition of literacy he had previously applied to his classroom. Reflecting on our class discussion, he noted that "literacy is not simply something that you can judge to be 'there' or 'absent' in a student." These counter-narratives suggest that certain course assignments and subsequent opportunities for ongoing reflection can help corps members identify and problematize their assumptions regarding student achievement. Finally, in discussing her assumptions about student achievement, Erica wrote:

> I, too, am guilty of identifying my students by their guided reading group name. The Blueberries are my lowest leveled readers. I often catch myself talking about how I don't know how to help the "Blueberries." Once, when talking about a student who jumped from the lowest level reading group to the middle reading group, my co-teacher said, "That's pretty good for a Blueberry!" The name "Blueberry" now connotes low readers who need extra help. Each student in that group is classified with that low-performing academic identity.

In reflecting upon her use of the term "Blueberry," Erica recognized how quickly categories of achievement were translated into lasting identities (Rist, 1970/2000). Thus, corps members' assumptions regarding their students' abilities have significant bearing on the future achievement of those students. Research has shown that if students are continually viewed by educators as low achieving or incapable, they will begin to adopt and enact these identities, making the chances of mainstream success more remote (Fordham, 1999; Gibson & Hidalgo, 2009; Gitlin, Buendia, Crosland, & Doumbia, 2003).

In her article "'You Save My Life Today, but for What Tomorrow?' Some Moral Dilemmas in Humanitarian Aid," Mary Anderson (1998) speaks to this problematic depiction of those one is seeking to help:

> As they [aid workers] sit around talking in the evening, conversation frequently involves stories of dangers encountered, local people outsmarted, would-be thieves caught. Tales are told of weaknesses, failures, and shortcomings of local people and local systems that have to be dealt with by the superior knowledge/intelligence/wisdom of outside agencies or personnel. (p. 151)

In attempting to explain how aid workers come to resent the very people who drew them to the work in the first place, Anderson (1998) suggests that "the process of distancing as an outsider from victim insiders very often represents a way of dealing with inequality" (p. 151). The honest questions raised in many of the vignettes support this notion, suggesting that corps members were using the assignment not only to contend with the practical challenges related to teaching but also to grapple with educational inequities writ large.

The vignettes also revealed that in countless instances, students were "framed" for the corps members beforehand by both TFA and Excel as low achievers, perhaps influencing these initial, problematic conceptions. For example, one corps member wrote:

> Leading up to the first day of school, Teach For America and [Excel] people—recruiters, advisors, mentors—kept telling me that I won't fully understand how far behind my future students are until I meet them. I took this to mean that perhaps a few students wouldn't know their letters, but that most of them would at least know basic words like dog and cat. On Friday of last week, I realized how wrong I was, and how much I underestimated what "behind" really means.

Another corps member, Wendy, was aware of the "deprivation framework" she brought to her teaching but felt as though it was reinforced not only by Teach For America but also by society at large, the school she worked in and even her students:

> The differences in "received understandings" and "perceived understandings" have serious implications on the psyche of an urban teacher. I receive the ideas of deprivation from society, from the school system and from individuals within the school—including my students.

Some of this framing occurred during the Teach For America Summer Institute, the five-week training program which all corps members participate in prior to entering the urban classroom. The manual distributed to corps members to prepare them to teach literacy establishes a "genre of crisis" by citing an array of demoralizing statistics, the most startling of which is the claim that 74% of students enter first grade "at risk" for school failure (Teach For America, 2007, p. 12). However, the document is quick to make the distinction that not all American students are at risk for school failure. Rather it is the poor, minority students who are consistently testing below basic levels as children and subsequently re-appearing in the prison system as illiterate teenagers. While the TFA materials mention the need for print-rich early literacy environments to support these students, the document also asserts that students are deprived of rich literacy experiences before they even arrive in school. For example, they cite the Hart and Risley (1995) vocabulary study which asserts that poor children come to school with a deficit of nearly 30 million words, an educational starting point which does not bode well for the rest of their academic career.

Corps members further struggled to reconcile these images of students with their perceptions of their role as educators. In some instances, for example, depictions of students as "deficient" influenced how teachers conceived of their job. For example, Melinda wrote, "Overwhelmed by statistics about my students' minimal proficiencies, I felt it my job to swoop in with ideas and impart knowledge." If Melinda had anticipated bright students with a range of capacities, she may have adopted different pedagogical and philosophical stances towards her instruction. Instead, she adopted what Freire (1970) referred to as the "banking model" of education in which students are positioned as passive recipients rather than co-creators of knowledge.

In addition to the depictions of students as at academically low levels or deficient, families, school administrations and veteran teachers were also framed in advance as incompetent or uncaring, leading corps members to make assumptions regarding both their own responsibilities as teachers and the urban contexts they entered. When Eleanor, for example, discovered that her school housed a supportive administration and excellent veteran teachers, she reflected angrily on what she was prepared to expect:

> I love my students. I love my administration. They're really supportive and are working hard for the students and their education, which is something I didn't expect from what TFA told me I would get, which is ridiculous. It just makes me so mad, this type of brainwashing TFA tried to do with these five weeks during Institute to prepare me for what I was going to do. . . . That only TFA can teach students and be prepared, because you're not going to have very much support from your administration. The other teachers are going to be mean. That hasn't been my experience at all.

Eleanor discovered that her actual experience teaching in an urban environment was distinctly at odds with the expectations outlined by Teach For America. Though TFA clearly extols the importance good teachers can make in the lives of students, Eleanor was not encouraged to draw upon the veteran teachers at her school, who turned out to be excellent resources:

> There's a first-grade teacher and this is her third year of teaching and she's become one of my good friends, because she's been so supportive of my teaching. She's a great teacher. I go to her for everything I need help on. I've seen her teach. We teach social studies and science together so we can switch off and have a break. She's a great teacher. I didn't expect anybody else to be a great teacher unless you were TFA because that's

what I had been told, which is totally ridiculous. The fact that our school is full of great teachers who are working really hard and they are not TFA; they are teachers who really care and this is what they want to do. They don't just want to do it for two years. They want to do it for their life. That's where TFA has a lot of stuff wrong.

While TFA might have been aiming to prepare teachers to work in challenging and isolating settings, many teachers found the framing problematic as they entered the field with diminished expectations regarding the kinds of support they might encounter and the caliber of their colleagues. Moreover, others felt that TFA encouraged an inflated sense of their own importance as teachers. Denis, for example, noted the following regarding his changing beliefs about the formative role of teachers in urban school contexts:

> Before actually starting to teach, the assumption was that I was going to provide that support for kids that might not otherwise have it. Now I feel like my understanding of where that support comes from is different. It can come from so many different places. The teacher might not be as formative. . . . I think teachers are formative, but they might not be as central as it was presented when I was applying to TFA.

In explaining how he came to these new understandings, Denis mentioned conducting home visits for each of his students and, in so doing, realizing the kinds of extensive support their families provided. Denis found that the parents had hopes and dreams for their children and were working daily to support school learning:

> One of the questions that I would ask at each visit was, "What are your dreams for your child and how do you see yourself helping your child in school?" [There is a prevalent belief] that these parents can't because they are so busy and they have to make ends meet. They are very limited in their involvement. They are necessarily limited in their involvement because of the conditions in which they work and that's why they can't be a helpful resource. There are a lot of progressive people and a lot of progressive thinkers that still hold that view because it does not seem wrong and it makes sense.

Interestingly, the decision to make a home visit to families was not something mandated by Teach For America or suggested by the charter school in which he worked but rather a decision Denis made to gather data for a new literacy initiative he planned to launch in his free time. These visits allowed Denis to move beyond the more limiting narratives of parent involvement and to transcend discourses that frame parents as incapable or uncaring. Instead, by conducting home visits, Denis was able to gauge how much parents were already doing in the service of their children:

It's kind of intuitive, so it was helpful to go on home visits and ask the parents those two questions. It was really moving to see how they spoke about it. There weren't a ton of parents that really had to think, "Hmmm. What are my dreams for my kids?" They had a pretty concrete and strong vision and they still really passionately do that and a lot of them are like, "I want my kid to be doing better than I'm doing now. I want my kid to do this, that and the other." It's something that they have put a lot of thought and energy into already. The next question was, "How do you see yourself helping your child?" So many parents volunteered things that they are already doing. I asked that question hoping to start the brainstorm with them things they could do to help, but what I got was them telling me what they were already doing. A lot of them were putting a lot of time and energy into it whether it was directly or a grandparent, a lot of kids reading at home. They would say, "At the supermarket, I pick up these books and read with my kid at night."

Unfortunately, the conception of urban students being exceptionally "low" level or "behind" is so entrenched in public consciousness that there seems to be little space in which teachers, like Denis, might discover other possibilities. In an analogous example from the aid industry, Anderson (1998) mentions that the humanitarian community has come to rely on "needs assessments" rather than "capacities assessments" before beginning work in a particular community: "A capacities assessment communicates respect for people's competence, their skills in life management, and their minds and spirits" (p. 142). She suggests that applying a capacities rather than needs-based framework might prove effective in re-framing how "victims" are viewed and the ways in which work in impoverished communities is approached, conducted and disseminated.

Blame

Corps members face a dilemma as they attempt to assign blame for what many consider the profound underachievement of their students. According to Denis, when corps members must contend with their own limitations as educators, it produces a desire/tendency to assign blame, "Because then people are like, 'I don't know how to teach. Who do I point my finger at?'" Like aid workers "who experience the limits of their effectiveness as a kind of failure—a failure which begets guilt, which begets blame: blame at the government, at the bureaucracy of their organization, even at the aid recipients themselves" (Dawes, 2007, pp. 148–149), corps members are also seeking an explanation for their exceptionally trying and exhausting circumstances. As with aid workers, corps members vary in how they assign blame. Families and communities are certainly pinpointed as potentially negative influences on students. One corps member stated the following with regards to how families can determine the educational outcomes of their children:

> The amount that the family interacts and the way in which this interaction plays out either sets children up to be successful readers, or puts them at a distinct disadvantage from day one of Kindergarten. Many of my first-graders at [my] school in [Ridgeville] fall into the latter of these two categories. They are unable to read short sentences or follow the pattern of a simple text.

Another corps member who worked almost exclusively with students from Spanish-speaking families described her students' families and communities by writing, "These students who speak exclusively Spanish in their home, often times living with parents and relatives who can neither read or write in English, are essentially coming into their Americanized educational experience completely blind." This corps member worried that her students' families' inability to speak fluent English compromised the potential for student achievement. In a similar statement, Cynthia blamed a family's use of non-Standard English as a factor impeding the academic success of her pre-K students:

> Through the day, many of my students speak grammatically incorrect [sic]. For example, instead of saying "I have a red shirt," they say "I got a red shirt." . . . Grammatically incorrect speech is modeled to my students in their home and community. It seems they are so accustomed to speaking this way, they are not receptive to change.

Once again, language—in this case the use of non-Standard English—is viewed as worrisome rather than framed as a capacity to be built upon. Moreover, Cynthia went on to state that "this speech will likely have negative implications on my students' future including how they are perceived and possibly their academic success." Cynthia was thus concerned that family and community language would limit the future prospects of her students.

Corps members also blamed themselves and their own perceived inadequacies as educators for certain facets of student underachievement. Christa, who previously discussed her students' Spanish-language abilities, cited her classroom management shortcomings as the reason her students struggled to achieve. In lamenting her inability to meet the needs of attentive students who came to school hoping to learn, Christa wrote, "While these students could be grasping the intricacies of scientific or mathematical language, they are instead surrounded by the constant chatter (in both English and Spanish) and inundated by the disruptions of students who should have been removed from the classroom long ago." Here Christa acknowledged her own classroom management failures but she also placed at least some of the blame on a school or system that should have removed certain students from the classroom long ago. Thus Christa implied that if certain students were removed, other children would achieve at higher levels. Similarly, in a written course assignment, Nicolas referred to himself as "the worst, most insensitive teacher in the world" for losing patience with a student who he realized later did not know how to read. While these admissions of teacher shortcomings and insensitivity are powerful, they are still coupled with a depiction of students as incapable and academically deficient—depictions which ironically undermine the very work the corps members are meant to do.

Infinite Jurisdiction and Control

Generally speaking, corps members and aid workers enter their respective fields with a desire to improve people's life chances. The corps members I worked with had obvious concerns regarding the future prospects of their students; both Teach For America and Excel place a premium on college attendance as a significant indicator of success, a notion which is emphasized beginning in pre-K. The term "infinite jurisdiction," employed by Tanya, a second-grade Excel teacher, when I was observing in her classroom is a useful metaphor for theorizing the ways in which some corps members understand their mission to promote the academic achievement of their students. According to Tanya, "infinite jurisdiction" is a term used by the Excel Charter Network to signify that the teacher's control must extend beyond the confines of the classroom. Tanya, for example, was expected to maintain control over the hallways outside her classroom even if it meant disciplining children whom she did not know. The overt use of this language invites an exploration into how far the jurisdiction of the school should extend in the service of promoting student achievement and whether students' homes and futures are subject to school policies. In yet another parallel to the aid industry, Rony Brauman, former president of Médecins Sans Frontières (MSF), notes, "What the people we help do in the future is not our business unless we feel we want to go back to colonial times where we order their lives. If we are dealing with equals they should be able to write their own history and their own future" (as cited in Dawes, 2007, p. 208). This notion can be a difficult one to fully embrace when one of the explicit purposes of both aid work and urban education entails improving the life chances of certain constituencies. Yet, Brauman's invocation of colonialism underscores the web of complexity surrounding college rhetoric. Again, like aid workers, corps members must wrestle with issues of control and must reconcile their hopes for their students' future with other, contradictory narratives.

Concerns about students' futures manifested themselves in a number of different ways and began to surface even at the early elementary grades. Though she could have selected any topic, Esther designed a unit on college for her first-grade students which featured, as a capstone project, the writing of a predictive autobiography in which students were to explicitly map out a path to college. Other elements of the unit included a tour of a college campus and the perusal of college materials in order to identify potential majors. After completing the unit, Esther reflected on whether it was a developmentally appropriate activity to engage in with her students:

> In reflection, I also consider to what extent it is appropriate to push a college-bound agenda as early in a child's educational career as I did, and I wonder whether or not I will change my mind in this regard over the course of the upcoming years.

Esther was not unique in her desire to introduce ideas about college attendance to her young students. All of the teachers featured in the study are elementary school teachers and many of them used the class assignments as a means for expressing concern regarding students' perceived trajectories or designed activities meant to help their students plan for and envision alternate futures. Corps members viewed these discourses about the future as a source of motivation for their students; many believed, for example, that if the connection between literacy achievement and college attendance were made explicit, students would show increased motivation:

> Overall, my interviews showed me that my students are generally passionate about reading. They are able to make vague connections between reading, school, increasing knowledge and future prospects. My goal is to make these connections more concrete to increase their drive.

Frustrated with their inability to directly influence the home lives and experiences of their students, some corps members were determined to focus increased energy on the classroom. For example, in conducting interviews regarding his students' home literacy practices, Jason worried that his first-grade students were not actually reading at home but merely "flipping through books." Wrestling with his prospective reach as an educator, Jason began to feel that meaningful learning could occur only in the classroom where he managed to maintain a great deal of control:

> These questions also made me realize that I need to work within my own locus of control. I cannot control what goes on at each of my students' homes. The only thing that I can control is what we do in the classroom. With this in mind it is my job to take the information I learned from these questions and use it in a way to help foster each student's growth as a reader.

In a similar questioning of home literacy practices and commensurate effort to increase what is possible in the classroom setting, Melissa stated the following:

> Based on what I have learned from my students, I can gather that the home environment is not the best for reading. In my reading group, therefore, I need to foster the type of environment that they do not encounter at home; it needs to be calm, quiet and focused on allowing students to sound out the words and write the words on their own.

Moreover, a kindergarten teacher named Deneah expressed concerns about how the attitudes of her students' parents and the kinds of activities conducted in the home sphere would affect the future achievement of her students. In a vignette composed for class, she related an anecdote about a parent who refused to fill out a reading log over the weekend because she preferred to do other activities with her children during this time. Deneah wrote:

> I began the conversation by restating her note and how reading was essential for her child's educational growth. I began to recite everything that I believed and everything that had been drilled into my head about my student's future. I spoke with such confidence and I was certain that her mother would believe what I was selling.

Deneah left the conversation with this parent feeling misunderstood and frustrated by the contrasting expectations and educational philosophies. Convinced of her mission through Teach For America to close the achievement gap and work toward equity, she could not see value in this mother's assertion that young children should participate in a range of different activities on the weekends. In another assignment, Deneah continued her contemplation of whether she and her students' families had the same agenda with regards to achievement: "As Rachel sat describing books she read and her reading practices, I could not help but wonder if her mother realized how crucial reading is to her child's success." Just as students were broadly depicted as underachieving, families were often described as unable or unwilling to help children achieve significant academic goals.

While teachers like Deneah espoused personal convictions regarding their students' future achievement, for many teachers, the ongoing reinforcement of college rhetoric was mandated by their schools. Excel teachers, for example, were evaluated on how effectively they incorporated "success speak" into their lessons. In this discussion, Barbara and Daphne, two early childhood teachers, problematized Excel's overwhelming emphasis on college:

> Daphne: I got "Developing" on my last formal [evaluation] because I didn't have enough success speak in my lesson. I was told to reference the blue book in my formal debrief to get examples and one of them was something about college. It was applicable to high-schoolers. Those are the examples in the blue book. "You guys are doing such a good job and some kind of reference to . . ."

> Barbara: "We're going to get to college. If you get this lesson today, it will help you get to college."

> Daphne: I get in trouble because that stuff doesn't come out of my mouth ever.

> Barbara: "If you don't do this worksheet, you're not getting into college."

Like Esther, then, these two teachers pondered the appropriateness of motivating kindergarten and first-grade students through a discourse focused on the distant and remote notion of college attendance. However, due to Excel's intense focus on higher education, teachers have little choice but to conform to this way of speaking, lest they risk repeated poor evaluations or possibly even termination. Indeed, the Excel teacher handbook outlines specific guidelines regarding what it refers to not as "success speak," as the teachers call it, but as "Speak Success":

> If you say anything frequently enough, people start to believe it! This is the idea behind Speak Success. Specifically, if a teacher tells students that they will achieve, ultimately students start to believe it and their actions follow suit. It's the positive spin of a self-fulfilling prophesy.

This is not to suggest that holding high expectations for students is not essential or that students shouldn't be encouraged to set and attain worthwhile goals; rather, the teacher's hopes for the students' futures could be contextualized in light of the broader social/economic/political/cultural forces that have conspired to minimize the presence of low-income, minority students in higher education. Structural challenges that might inhibit the future achievement of students are notably absent from the discourse of the corps members who focus instead on the efforts and capabilities of the individual. Many corps members did recognize, however, that the extensive emphasis on college began to function as a mechanism for control which could actually impede student chances for academic success:

> I grapple with this all the time or I look at my students and I forget they are elementary school kids, because they are treated like little adults at our school and I don't think that's the best way. I think that's kind of where it's holding them down where they're not having that time to try different areas, because not everyone excels at academics. There could be a student that we're holding back from being a musical genius. . . . I just feel like they're set in that trap where you have to go to college. Do well at this school so you can go to a good high school and go to college. So we are kind of holding back other areas that they may excel at.

Not only are college attendance and future success wielded as controlling mechanisms, but also there is evidence that while students internalize the rhetoric to some degree, for many of them it is divorced from authentic learning and otherwise devoid of meaning. In describing a conversation with his third-grade students, Nicolas noted the following:

> Also central to [Excel's] ideology is college rhetoric. Starting in kindergarten the purpose of school is defined as college attendance; each classroom is named after a college and grade levels are often defined as their graduating college class. (Third grade is the Class of 2024, for instance.) I was interested in how the combination of stressing reading and college acceptance impacted how students perceived the purpose of reading. Interestingly, all three students directly tied reading to college and later success. Laniya and Nigel both said that reading was important because "you need to know a lot of words to go to college." Xavier's response demonstrated a brutal honesty and cynicism: "So you can go to college and get a good job. Other than that, it's corny."

Here Nicolas illustrated that while the rhetoric has indeed pervaded the consciousness of his students, reading retained little meaning for them in and of itself. Students' parents, siblings and other family members likely use literacy for a range of daily purposes like reading for pleasure, storytelling, completing household tasks, communicating with extended family and friends in other locations (Heath, 1983). However, when these literacy practices are ignored by schools and the broader purpose of literacy is narrowed to college attendance, educators miss an opportunity to make important home/school connections and to build upon children's cultural knowledge and capacities (Campano, 2008; Moll, Amanti, Neff, & Gonzáles, 2005).

Undergirding the discourse of future achievement and college attendance is the notion that leaving the neighborhood behind is one of the implicit by-products of academic success. As Popkewitz (1998) notes, "Historically, the focus on urban and rural schools is part of a larger trajectory of school reform capturing a 19th century view of schooling as a means to rescue children from their economic, social and cultural conditions through planned intervention" (p. 21). Numerous corps members struggled with the assumption that future success implies abandoning home communities. As Moll and González (1997) note, home communities are often viewed "as places from which children must be saved or rescued, rather than places that, in addition to problems (as in all communities), contain valuable knowledge and experiences" (p. 98). In lamenting the messages communicated by her school regarding college attendance and the role she played in "saving" students from their current circumstances, one corps member stated the following:

> I have a really big problem with our school because it's set up so that the curriculum holds all of the knowledge and we are people who are transmitting it to our students and our students are taught, "You sit still and silent, you have your eyes on the teacher and you better not move, because if you don't, you're not going to get that information, you're not going to go to college and you're not going to get out of this neighborhood." That's the message that is put through our school. It's like, "This school is coming here and they are going to save you. This school has the information and we know the one straight path to college.

Like Nicolas, this corps member struggled with the notion that hopes for future achievement remained divorced from deeper meaning and a commitment to actual learning and were based instead on notions of obedience and conformity:

> College isn't about learning and college isn't about gaining knowledge and becoming a leader. It's about being obedient and getting credentials so you can get a job and get money and get out of [the neighborhood]. That for me is hands down the biggest struggle that I have every day. Personally, every day I'm like, "What the hell am I doing?" I am telling kids, "The only way you will be successful is if you listen to me and you better not dare interrupt me because I will call your mother and tell her that you were bad in school. Then you're not going to go to college." Why is my kindergartener telling me, "I am sitting like a star right now so my brain with grow and I can graduate college"? That's really upsetting for me. They don't even know what college is, but it's this arbitrary thing that they are going to get. None of it's about learning.

Some corps members chose to respond to these troubling messages by designing units for the course that would emphasize the positive aspects of the students' communities in an effort to emphasize the problematic aspects of encouraging an escape-mentality. Moreover, these units aimed to draw upon community resources in order to encourage deeper learning. One corps member was particularly inspired by what she considered a troubling emphasis on college as a means of escape and wrote the following in the rationale for her unit, which emphasized the broad range of assets presented in the community:

> Since the beginning of the year, our school has had a "going to college" theme which has given our students a concrete reason to be successful in grades kindergarten through twelve. While this is a wonderful reason, I feel that the overarching college theme simultaneously passes on the message that escaping from their local, urban communities is their ultimate goal. Most of our students have lived in their community all of their lives with their families and their extended families nearby. The neighborhood is where they have had most new experiences and shaped their perspectives. It is a place rich as any other community with culture and should not be a place from which our students should "escape" if given the chance.

In executing these units which were intended to draw upon community resources and knowledge, some corps members discovered troubling insights with regards to how the children viewed their communities and, by extension, themselves. Though corps members planned lessons and activities that would connect the mandated curriculum to their students' lived experiences in the neighborhood, in several instances, these lessons seemed to perpetuate rather than interrupt stereotypes regarding the community. For example, Christa wrote the following:

> I encouraged them to use whatever adjectives they wanted so that we could continue our focus on neighborhood transformation and an exploration of their culture. The adjectives that they listed were surprisingly negative: scary, loud, dangerous, ghetto, crazy, energetic, friendly. I then asked the students to give reasons to support the adjectives that they listed. Their neighborhood was dangerous because "people rob each other, sell drugs, kill each other for no reason and have loud parties." Among the positive adjectives, students listed that "kids are always playing outside in the streets, people are always talking and friendly with each other." It was interesting to see that without any prompting or leading questions the students chose overwhelmingly negative adjectives when simply asked to describe their neighborhood. Although it was refreshing to see so many students engaged in the lesson, I did have the fear that by writing these adjectives on the board I was reaffirming to the children that the place that they lived truly was bad.

One of the most challenging aspects of inviting corps members to put the community at the center of their curriculum and pedagogy occurred when their students shared about what Zipin (2009) refers to as dark funds of knowledge. In his study with Australian educators, Zipin found that many were hesitant to join dark funds of knowledge with the formal curriculum, believing that issues related to drugs, violence and so on do not belong in classroom discourse. While attending to these concerns could reinforce stereotypes of students and their communities, Zipin emphasizes the importance of consistently negotiating the tension which exists between encouraging educators to view urban neighborhoods from an asset-based perspective while simultaneously recognizing the real structural constraints which exist in these settings (Buck & Skilton-Sylvester, 2005). As an instructor, I discovered that it was not adequate to merely ask teachers like Christa to bring their students' experiences into the classroom; I also needed to provide her with the language and frameworks necessary for considering how these experiences exist within and alongside broader, structural issues.

Brooke, a corps member who chose to explore language use within the social studies unit she designed, was aware that the ways in which her students perceived their hybrid language uses in many ways reflected the ways in which languages have been historically positioned and privileged within the United States. To help students identify the ways in which their own language practices were typically marginalized in mainstream society, Brooke designed a case study which asked students to consider the historical and geographic roots of the Creole language and its subsequent marginalization. It was Brooke's hope that a close examination of Creole would prompt connections to the students' own experiences as "hybrid" language speakers who draw upon Spanish, African American Vernacular English (AAVE), Standard English and other communicative resources. However, Brooke's third-graders struggled to translate the Creole case study to their own personal experiences with language:

> As far as I was able to get with my students in this unit, I felt like their insights definitely surprised me. . . . The marginalization of their culture is so severe that even they neglect to see value in it automatically all of the time. Even though I'm a white teacher who had the privilege never to consider these issues as a third-grader, I was able to create an environment where kids could question the differences between how we speak and how we write. They automatically said that Creole people and slaves were no different or worse than the American people, but they hesitated when they had to consider themselves and the way that they speak.

These data suggest that addressing student underachievement is more complex than raising standardized test scores and involves finding ways to help students adopt a critical stance on their learning. When literacy is conceived of as an autonomous set of skills which can be transferred easily from one setting to another, issues like internalized oppression, sociocultural context and criticality are effectively ignored

Remaining in/Leaving the Urban Classroom

Helping professions like social work and teaching have always been characterized by high rates of attrition and burnout. Questions of leaving, however, are considered differently within Teach For America primarily because corps members are asked to commit only to two years in the urban classroom and it is now widely assumed that the majority will move on after those two years to pursue other careers. While some studies have found that up to 60% of TFA corps members continue beyond their two-year commitment, by the fourth year only an estimated 14% remain in their original placement (Donaldson & Moore-Johnson, 2011). Moreover, their long-term intentions prior to entering TFA have an impact on whether they remain teaching. Those who intend to make teaching a career or who majored in education as undergraduates are significantly more likely to remain in the classroom. Some corps members who entered the classroom with the intention of pursuing a career in education still found themselves unable to complete their tenure and made the difficult decision to leave in the middle of the year (Donaldson & Moore-Johnson, 2011).

According to Dawes (2007), international aid workers, like corps members, must accept that "their personal sacrifices will never make the difference they desired and they always learn this, early on—the despair can be as correspondingly profound as the hope, and can make continuing the work impossible" (p. 148). Indeed, several of the corps members involved in this study decided to leave the program early. Many others admitted to writing resignation letters but ultimately chose to stay—at least until the end of the year. One corps member, Eleanor, who did decide to leave midyear, went through a long and drawn-out decision-making process. Her account demonstrates that the decision to quit is often accompanied by intense feelings of guilt:

> I first interacted with my program director. He came to the school and I told him I had made a decision to leave and he basically told me it was the worst decision I could ever make. I needed to think about it more. He didn't accept the fact that I had already

talked to people who really knew me. He was very offended and told me so. He took it personally that I had not involved him in this decision. I was like, "It's a personal decision. You're not involved in my personal life and I don't need to talk to you about personal things."

Unlike some of the other corps members who chose to leave, Eleanor's decision was not the result of frustrations with her students, school or administration. Rather, she came to resent her program director's admonitions that no one else would want to teach her students. She assumed that he aimed to make her feel "bad" or guilty:

I was really disappointed in his distrust and disregard for my school. Nobody else wants to teach kids in west [Ridgeville]. He said that. He said, "It's not like there are people lined up to teach kids in west [Ridgeville]. They are just going to hire a long-term sub." He took it personally because somebody else has already quit and they are down to two teachers in the first grade at the same school. It was rude and it made me more angry than feel bad. It just made me angry. I totally lost a lot of respect for that individual as well as for TFA as a whole. Then I talked to another lady and I don't exactly know what her role is, but she's involved in a lot of stuff. She basically told me that it's not okay to leave kids in the middle of the year. I don't even remember. I just sat quiet while I was on the phone with her and at the end I said, "Okay." Then she went on to tell me some other stuff. She said, "Did you want to respond to what I said earlier?" I was like, "Not really. I've heard it before. What do you want me to do, argue with you about it?" It just made me angry. I was like, "I'm not even going to waste my time on this."

Though Eleanor clearly had some mixed feelings regarding her decision, she was not persuaded to stay by TFA's efforts and followed through with her decision to leave the classroom in mid-October. Another corps member, Annika, also ended up quitting but waited until the end of the school year out of concern for the well-being of her students:

I didn't quit in the middle of the year. I am going to see my kids through the end of the year. There was a point where I felt like I was going to quit. I knew that I would feel worse for longer. I knew how bad I was feeling in November. I would feel worse so much longer if I left my kids at that point of the year. I knew that would have been so much worse. I definitely stayed the year because of my students. I don't know if I'm quitting because of TFA. I don't know. It has not been a good match.

Interestingly, Annika did not entirely give up on teaching, professing plans to teach again in the future but felt as though teaching through TFA was not the right fit for her. She seemed to justify a difficult decision through her assertion that staying through the end of the year made a difference to her students. Even those teachers who decided to remain in the classroom for the duration of their two-year commitment entertained thoughts and fantasies of quitting. Micah, for example, like Annika, cited the desire not to abandon his students in the middle of the year as one of his primary reasons for staying, even though he did not feel particularly successful as an educator:

> They [the students] might get on my nerves and I could be so annoyed with them, but at the same time, like I can find a reason for all my students why I love them and why I want to go back there every day. They have too many changes. I have thought many times in the year to quit. I think everybody has, at that school especially, but they are just going through so many changes that it is not going to be helpful to have another change in their life. Just being there I figure is consistency. Even if I am not teaching well or they are not learning a lot, at least consistency will help.

One recurring narrative involves the notion that students need consistency above all else and that an unskilled teacher who cares deeply about students is most likely superior to a long-term sub, which is how most teachers conceive of the alternative. Alex, however, expressed doubts about whether the consistency that corps members provided was really superior to the possible alternative:

> I think by October, people start quitting and it gets very rough because they get really overwhelmed. You are just not prepared. You are just given a really good pep talk and you're doing a really good thing so go in there and try your best. I think we're doing more harm than good.

Of the many corps members asked about their desire to leave the urban classroom, Alex was the only person to express the sentiment that his presence with his students was ultimately causing more harm than good. Debates around international aid and humanitarian intervention reflect Alex's concerns regarding whether more harm than good is being accomplished. In her book *The Crisis Caravan*, for example, Linda Polman (2011) documents the ways in which humanitarian assistance has fueled international conflict. According to Polman, Westerners with limited understanding of places like Sierra Leone and Rwanda have prolonged human suffering through the misappropriation of goods and services. Similarly, authors like Darling-Hammond (1994) and Popkewitz (1998) worry that the framework of "normativity" which many corps members unknowingly apply to the urban and rural settings in which they work can severely compromise their ability to "help." In spite of such critiques, most corps members favor the narrative that the consistency they provide by remaining in a situation that is daunting and challenging offers the possibility for transformation. It's this narrative that allows teachers to continue working despite the perceived complications and hopelessness of a particular situation.

Conclusion

The application of a humanitarian lens to urban school reform is useful in illuminating the kinds of tensions that emerge when young teachers attempt to fulfill their mission of remedying educational inequities. Their desire, for example, to affect positively the life chances of students can lead to an atmosphere characterized by excessive control which limits rather than broadens student potential

The humanitarian aid industry is rife with examples of how top-down, cavalier endeavors have worsened the situation of various constituencies (Easterly, 2006; Polman, 2011). Similarly, the Teach For America model, characterized by short tenures in urban communities, rudimentary training and the omission of robust cross-cultural preparation, is strikingly similar to the kind of international development that tends to be least effective in the long term. As with humanitarian aid, one of the challenges of urban education is to effectively address the gravity of the problems without reifying problematic images of urban schools, students and families. This struggle proved to be particularly salient for corps members who struggled to dismiss deficit frameworks when discussing or writing about students, families and communities. Even when course assignments or discussion topics were left purposefully vague, issues of equity were raised again and again as corps members attempted to reconcile their expectations for urban teaching with the realities of their situations.

Although I aimed to offer a space of shared inquiry in which corps members could collaboratively problematize issues related to equity, diversity and achievement, some TFA teachers still found their work in urban classrooms untenable and, as a result, made the difficult decision to leave. Regardless of their decision, corps members continued to wrestle with their experiences and construct narratives about urban education as a means of sense-making. In understanding and assessing school reform initiatives like Teach For America whose primary aim is to eliminate the achievement gap, it is imperative to consider the perspectives of the teachers who are expected to carry out the work on a daily basis with few sanctioned spaces in which to theorize their own emerging ideas regarding urban schooling.

Chapter 5

"WE DON'T KNOW HOW TO BE TEACHERS": NEGOTIATING KNOWLEDGE AND PRACTICE IN THE ELEMENTARY CLASSROOM

In addition to problematic narratives about children, families and communities, which at times compromised their ability to construct productive learning environments, for their students, corps members often doubted their educational knowledge and teaching capacities and thus deferred to the expertise of their curricular resources even when they viewed these materials as limited or problematic. Further, while the discourse of Teach For America typically describes corps members as bright and capable leaders who have the desire and ability to positively affect schools, these teachers were sent contradictory messages within the context of Ridgeville as they were primarily positioned as passive rule followers required to implement prescriptive instructional programs. Similarly, although I aimed to use the course as a venue through which to introduce corps members to a range of relevant data sources, including classroom-based data, corps members struggled to view qualitative data as a valid source of knowledge, perhaps as the result of the emphasis that institutions like TFA, Excel and the school district placed upon quantitative measures to assess students and evaluate teachers. Ultimately, the corps members' espoused lack of educational knowledge made it difficult for them to actively resist dehumanizing policies, interrupt limited images of teaching and question the reliance on quantitative measures.

Epistemological concerns are integral to any conversation about teaching and learning, specifically in an era of school reform which favors a reductionist-model of knowledge. Foucault used the term "epistemes of knowledge" to theorize the dominant discourse of a particular time period. Rather than framing history as an overarching narrative of progress and achievement, Foucault examined changing patterns of discourse with attention to how power is manifested (as cited in Morrell, 2008). The current "episteme of knowledge" within the realm of education reform—characterized by high levels of standard-ization, widespread testing and a back-to-basics approach to instruction—has largely been shaped by the NCLB legislation (Cochran-Smith & Lytle, 2006). The Ridgeville corps members both came of age and entered teaching during a time period in which educational discourse emphasized the cumbersome requirements of traditional teacher education programs and promoted subject matter knowledge and teaching techniques as the cornerstones of effective instruction. As a result, questions concerning knowledge were of paramount importance to corps members who were wrestling with their own sense of efficacy within a broader system that continually positioned them as passive recipients rather than as active creators of knowledge. In particular, corps members contended with the following questions: What is the relationship between data and knowledge? What kinds of educational data should be used to inform instructional decisions? What conceptions of teacher knowledge are promoted within local and national contexts? What does it mean to know students and to mobilize this knowledge in the interest of deeper learning? What does it mean to really know something? And last, what kinds of learning inspire deep engagement and motivation?

In framing epistemological concerns with regards to teaching, Cochran-Smith and Lytle (1999) theorize three conceptions of teacher learning: knowledge-for-practice, knowledge-in-practice and knowledge-of-practice. The first conception, knowledge-for-practice, is the pervasive model within teacher education and suggests that "knowing more" (content, pedagogy, research-based methodology) will lead to more effective practice. Moreover, this conception of teacher learning depends on the assumption that the knowledge necessary for teaching and learning is generated by researchers in university settings generally outside of the K–12 classroom. Drawing upon what Shulman (1987) refers to as "the knowledge base for teaching," Cochran-Smith and Lytle (1999) express concerns regarding what it might mean for university-based researchers to try and codify a knowledge base for teaching—a move towards uniformity that undermines the "local knowledge" that individual teachers possess (Cochran-Smith & Lytle, 1993). A "knowledge-for-practice" conception of teaching has significant implications for alternative pathway programs like Teach For America due to the brief training period required for teachers. In the case of TFA, corps members spend only five weeks preparing to enter the classroom and thus are introduced to a prescriptive, formulaic mode of lesson instruction presumably so that they will feel they know something about teaching and learning before entering urban classrooms. The materials used to prepare corps members to enter K–12 classrooms further the knowledge-for-practice conception of teacher learning. For example, the *Elementary Literacy Guide* used as the primary "textbook" during TFA Summer Institute (Teach For America, 2007) defines literacy as a set of autonomous skills transferable between contexts. Further, the teaching guide goes on to extol certain scientifically proven ways to teach reading and claims that an application of these research-based methods will enable students to decode and understand texts. Unfortunately, as Cochran-Smith and Lytle (1999) suggest, a knowledge-for-practice conception lends itself to a transmission model of teaching, one that essentially views both teachers and students as passive recipients rather than as active creators of knowledge. Finally, a knowledge-for-practice framework privileges empirical modes of knowing and a best-practices stance in which one best way of doing something can be identified through scientific research.

The second conception of teacher learning outlined by Cochran-Smith and Lytle (1999) is knowledge-in-practice, which they define as knowledge in action or the ways in which teachers draw upon ongoing, everyday circumstances to make important decisions about teaching. In the case of this framework, "the lines between knowledge generation and knowledge use are blurred" (p. 263). Knowledge-in-practice is occasionally described as "practical knowledge" and characterized by the ways in which teachers approach, consider and ultimately address classroom tensions and dilemmas. In other words, knowledge-in-practice is composed of the "wise action" that teachers are able to take in the midst of confusing or challenging circumstances (p. 266). Expertise, then, emerges from the teachers themselves, not solely from researchers or experts outside of the profession. Often this "practical" knowledge exists as part of an oversimplified dichotomy which places formal, content knowledge on one end of the spectrum and more practical, experiential knowledge on the other end.

The third conception of teacher learning outlined by the authors is knowledge-of-practice, which views knowledge as inherently problematic. According to Cochran-Smith and Lytle (1999), a knowledge-of-practice framework "stands in contrast to the idea that there are two distinct kinds of knowledge for teaching, one that is formal, in that it is produced following the conventions of social science research, and one that is practical, in that it is produced in the activity of teaching itself" (p. 273). Further this conception attempts to interrupt the idea that experienced teachers know more than novice teachers; rather, it assumes that both groups are in the practice of making knowledge problematic. Cochran-Smith and Lytle (1999) also foreground the collective construction of knowledge instead of an isolated view of individual knowledge typically favored within school and classroom settings. Equally central to this collaborative view of knowledge creation is a re-casting of the teacher as agent in the hopes of interrupting dominant narratives which depict teachers as powerless consumers of outside knowledge. In this sense, the knowledge-of-practice framework foregrounds the "critical" in emphasizing the role of power and authority within schools.

Similarly significant to a knowledge-of-practice framework are the alternative forms of data suggested by such an approach. Not only is student, family and community knowledge of paramount importance in this conception but within such a framework teachers are encouraged to generate and use their own data rather than rely solely on data generated by university researchers or other outside experts. As Cochran-Smith and Lytle (1999) write, "Furthermore, teachers and other participants in inquiry communities have been inventing new forms and frameworks of analysis and interpretation. Some of these forms and frameworks may look quite unfamiliar to those who are accustomed to the traditional modes of data collection and analysis entailed in most university-based research" (p. 279). Thus, teaching is re-conceptualized into a more agentive endeavor requiring collaboration, knowledge generation and social action—an image which has implications for TFA corps members who, though socialized in a system that favors a knowledge-for-practice perspective, express a desire for a deeper and more complex view of teaching and learning.

Data Use in Teaching and Learning

Believing that a knowledge-of-practice stance was a productive means for framing teacher learning, one of the goals within my methods courses was to explicitly invite corps members to adopt the identity of teacher-researchers within their classrooms; my hope was that generating their own unique and localized knowledge would complicate some of the circulating mainstream narratives regarding students and families. Further, I explicitly sought to broaden the conversation regarding what counts as learning in urban classrooms. Knowing that Teach For America relies almost exclusively upon quantitative measures to gauge student achievement, I invited corps members to conduct in-depth literacy interviews with a small sampling of students, believing the information gleaned from this experience would provide an alternate lens for understanding and learning about their students. As Oakes, Franke, Quartz, and Rogers (2002) note in their research on urban teacher education programs, "We have found that the idea of expert needs to be broadly construed to include not only guiding teachers, colleagues, and university faculty but also parents, community members, and the students themselves" (p. 230).

In addition to positioning students as experts, the aim of the assignment was to encourage the corps members to explore students' out-of-school literacy practices as well as to investigate their beliefs about school-based literacy. As Gibson (2005) asserts, "When students perceive that their teachers understand their lives outside of school and care about them as complex individuals, they are more likely to engage in the learning process" (p. 596). The corps members, however, were free to select the students to interview and to design questions they felt were pertinent and engaging. Still struggling to come to terms with what they viewed as student deficits in reading and writing, numerous corps members used the assignment as an opportunity to "compare" the habits of high-achieving and low-achieving students. Moreover, although the assignment was descriptive in nature, corps members used the information that students provided in order to make quantitative assertions about achievement. As Kagan (1992) notes, this phenomenon is not unique within teacher education settings: "Candidates tend to use the information provided in course work to confirm rather than to confront and correct their preexisting beliefs" (p. 154).

Cynthia, for example, compared the literacy practices of "high-achieving" and "low-achieving" pre-K students when she wrote the following:

> The first trend I noticed was in my students' response to the first question: Do you read at home? How often? On one hand, my two struggling students were either inconsistent in their answers or unable to answer. The one said she reads independently, which at the pre-K level consists of looking at letters and forming her own stories based on the illustrations. These students were unable to name their favorite stories or titled their favorite stories incorrectly. They either stated they did not enjoy reading or were unable to articulate why they enjoyed it aside from providing a basic summary of the story. One student said he practices writing his name at home; the other said she does not. Aside from literacy, their interests include toys, games and football.

While these "low-achieving" students were clearly using a range of literacy practices both at home and at school—such as reading independently, writing their names and providing a basic summary of the text—Cynthia used the interview data as a means of reinforcing her understanding of their low achievement—namely, that they didn't read or engage with texts at home.

Similarly, the responses of the "higher-achieving" students were seen as evidence supporting their academic talent and abilities:

> On the other hand, my two advanced students were consistent in saying they read at home and specifically stated they read all the time or every day. They read independently and also are read to. They were also able to name favorite books and the one student constantly references books he has read in everyday interactions. They both enjoy reading, but also were not able to articulate why. They both say they practice writing and spelling their names at home. Their general interests outside of reading include playing games, basketball, blocks and jumping jacks.

Like Cynthia, many corps members undertook the assignment with a set of assumptions regarding the correlation that might exist between reading level and home literacy practices. Moreover, in choosing whom to talk to for the assignment, nearly all corps members sorted their students by reading level and relied solely on these criteria for generating an interview sample. In the most troubling of cases, corps members used the data generated by the interviews to affirm their assumptions regarding their students' interests and abilities related to literacy. For example, in interviewing one of her "lower" first-grade readers about home literacy practices, Esther noted the following: "She said that she reads with her mother when she goes to bed and generally they read half a book each night. She says that she has been reading daily with her mother since she was a baby, but I am skeptical of this given that her reading level is so very low." Although she took a doubting stance to the self-reporting made by this first-grade student, when a "higher-achieving" student reported practicing reading at home each day, Esther readily accepted the data: "When I heard this, it was easy for me to believe because she is the type of student who is earnestly hard working but might not be the most naturally intelligent." Not only do these examples suggest that some corps members held troubling beliefs regarding student achievement, but that data generated by the conversations with students were viewed subjectively as something to be believed or dis-believed.

In a similar type of analysis, Wendy gleaned a number of insights about reading from her fourth-grade students including the fact that nearly all of them enjoyed reading in their free time and did so daily. Despite this finding and what it suggested about her students' interests and capacities, Wendy focused instead on her discovery that out of twenty students in her class, only two had ever received books as gifts and that very few could successfully name a newspaper or magazine, which, to Wendy, was an indication that "there are not very many reading materials for parents either." In this way, qualitative data collected through student interviews and meant to enrich portraits of students as literacy learners were used instead to reinforce the quantitative measures upon which Teach For America, the school district and the corps members themselves heavily relied. Although the qualitative data collected through the assignment were continually subject to a certain level of skepticism, test scores and reading levels were reported neutrally and seldom questioned.

However, in other instances, corps members did use the assignment and the resulting data to explore provocative questions and to complicate and disrupt some of their dominant conceptions of students. For example, although Jayna relied on reading level as her primary criterion for selecting students to interview, she stated her assumptions up front and used the data which emerged from her questioning to further refine her interview protocol. When posing a question regarding what students like to do in school, Jayna discovered that even her "higher" readers preferred using computers to reading and used this information to shape her inquiry into reading practices. Eventually, through targeted and thoughtful questioning, Jayna found that for many of her students reading had become a mechanized task disconnected from any broader or deeper meaning. This led Jayna to pose yet another provocative question: "Could there be a connection between seeing the importance in reading and being a good reader?" As a result of her inquiry into understanding the purposes of reading, Jayna was able to shape her curricular and pedagogical approaches to make literacy instruction more meaningful for her students.

In a parallel use of interview data, Joey surmised through his literacy interviews that the ways in which Excel tracked his third-grade students in all content areas ultimately impeded their literacy abilities, writing: "I believe that these interviews show that the tracking method used at my school is not working. . . . Furthermore, students in those classes fall into the role of being the low-level class." Through the process of collecting data about his teaching, Joey was able to identify an important structural problem at his school characterized by the heavy tracking of young students and subsequent isolation of "low-achieving" students. Although he did not feel as though he possessed the authority as a first-year teacher to speak up against these school-wide systems, his literacy inquiry allowed him to explore and critique some of the broader political problems that shaped his students' experiences.

Instead of selecting "low readers" to focus on and interview, Farrah chose to talk with a group of middle school girls whom she observed reading prodigiously at school. Farrah discovered that for these girls, who sought out reading in their free time, literacy was not specifically tied to some distant promise of future achievement even though college attendance was a central component of the school's mission. Rather, the girls said that they read as much as they did simply because it was fun. Like Jayna, Farrah's initial inquiry into literacy led her from one question to another. She ended her piece by asking, "Is being well-read as important as reading well?" Finally, Christa, who throughout the semester struggled to meet the needs of her Spanish-speaking students, used the literacy interview assignment as an opportunity to explore and understand language capacities. By exploring their language histories and asking questions about family language practices, Christa discovered that her students were, in fact, "incredibly intelligent" but had been tracked unfairly due to their lack of mastery over the English language:

> The questions that I asked my kids had to do with Spanish and English. All of them speak Spanish and speak English exclusively in school. A few of the lower readers learned to read and write in Spanish before they learned to read and write in English and then two of the higher ones learned to write in English before and they don't know how to read or write in Spanish. I thought that was interesting. These kids have been trapped into this lower track and they're in the lower group. They just don't get it because all of the benchmark tests and everything that is there to systematically track them doesn't gear to the fact that they're incredibly intelligent. They just don't speak English that great.

Like Joey, her inquiry into language invited new conceptions regarding her school and the structural bias which was evident in the relegation of Spanish-speaking students to lower-track classrooms.

For me as a course instructor, these varying responses to the literacy interview project posed some interesting dilemmas as the assignment was taken up, executed and interpreted in unexpected ways and in some instances did not provoke the kinds of insights I had expected. I struggled, then, to debrief these findings with the corps members. I required one corps member, for example, to revise her interview, noting some of the obvious deficit-laden language. She followed my directions and turned in a "new" paper, but it is doubtful that this "revision" represented any substantial shift in her viewpoints.

Although my courses invited corps members to draw upon alternative forms of data including the literacy interviews they conducted with students and the teacher-research accounts which made up some of the course reading, many questioned whether these alternate forms of "knowing" actually counted as research. For example, in responding to a course text, Campano's (2007) *Immigrant Students and Literacy*, which is a teacher-research account of working with immigrant students, Annette expressed concerns about how such an approach would translate to her more rigid school environment:

> This view of education is incredibly alluring to me. I wonder what instructor would not relish the opportunity to teach in such a free and nurturing environment. However, this is far from what my placement school expects me to do. I am encouraged to stay far away from this type of "activity" and instead rely on "real' measures of student growth such as data gained by answers to multiple choice questions.

Although Annette found aspects of Campano's approach "alluring" and expressed a desire to create a classroom that encouraged more creative and open-ended instruction, she worried about whether this kind of approach would actually produce the test results which her school required as evidence of successful teaching. She went on to ponder whether the data provided in his text can count as legitimate knowledge: "Should teachers and researchers publish actual studies with real data in order for school districts to take their conclusions seriously? Can longitudinal studies based on the individual stories of one teacher be generalized to make a change for the public?" While teacher researchers have struggled to have their work accepted within the Academy, the media, government institutions and other settings that have historically privileged empirical data, it is clear that teachers themselves wonder about the legitimacy of teacher research and feel more comfortable relying upon more "objective" measures to guide instructional practice.

Even when teachers like Annette found value in an account like Campano's, they wondered how they might introduce alternative ways of knowing into their classrooms in which one singular type of datum—the test score—was privileged over others. As Barbara noted:

> When I think about the curriculum and everyone complaining about it, I don't like Reading Mastery in particular, but how can we change it? How can we make them not use it anymore? What you can do is you can not use it now and you can do something that may or may not work. It's so data driven, like you can use it and show it doesn't work and then maybe they will actually change it if enough people come forward and say, "I actually did this every day and my kids did not learn letters and did not learn sounds." Then they might throw in something new like a new research based phonics program. Who knows? How do you win? You can not use it but then how do you know?

In this instance, Barbara was struggling fundamentally with what it means to "know" something about teaching and learning and what tools were at her disposal for convincing others. Interestingly, the term "data driven" as used here and by other corps members suggests that instruction should be informed by classroom data. What is not stated explicitly but is implied by the kinds of measures privileged in the school district and by TFA is that only quantitative measures should drive instruction. Barbara, for example, despite her reservations with regards to the Reading Mastery program, wondered how she might convincingly demonstrate the limitations of the program. Tanya had similar concerns but chose to resist what she deemed an overemphasis on quantitative measures by assigning grades arbitrarily and pursuing alternative instructional approaches:

> I've stopped giving assessments at the end of class. I make up grades and I put it into the computer, because they don't mean anything to me anyway. So, "Eh, this sounds about right." I just enter in something, because they're not actually looking at the work anyway. And I teach them what I want to teach them, because they like it, I like it, now we're talking about things. Now at school I ask them, "Tell me more about this thing," or they want to know. But they want something that's real and they know it's not that rinky-dink video about Martin Luther King.

Tanya's account suggests that her students' level of interest in the curriculum and willingness to engage with ideas were more important forms of data than a set of grades which can be arbitrarily assigned. Similarly, in a reflection for class, Annika considered the stark contrast between her own K–12 education, which was characterized by progressive pedagogy and experiential projects, with the kinds of assignments and activities she employed with her own students:

> I cannot remember a time when I was ever asked [in elementary school] to sit still, be quiet and listen to a teacher for hours on end. Yet I seem to be asking it of my students every single day. I have taken the parts of my curriculum that are least related to how I learned/learn and asked my students to feel engaged and excited by them. Tonight's conversation clarified for me how absurd that is and how much I am failing my students by doing so.

Like Tanya, Annika experienced dissonance in attempting to reconcile her beliefs about education with the kind of instructional program she found herself implementing on a daily basis. Both teachers were determined to find ways to resist the narrow conceptions of teaching and learning which were forced upon them. However, Tanya's and Annika's examples of resistance were exceptions among the corps members in my classes, most of whom contended that their inexperience as educators precluded them from speaking up or taking action even when they found certain curricular mandates or instructional approaches objectionable. No one, for example, other than Tanya, shared so openly regarding attempts to subvert systems of evaluation and accountability. Many doubted the value of their own localized knowledge as practitioners, believing that the outside researchers who had designed the curriculum or school leaders who orchestrated the instructional program should be deferred to at all costs.

Images of Teacher Knowledge

In theorizing aspects of teacher resistance and compliance, Achinstein and Ogawa (2006) illustrate how an assumed lack of knowledge about teaching makes the questioning of particular policies difficult for novice teachers who are entering schools or districts which are under intense pressure to bolster achievement levels. Corps members largely echoed these sentiments, insisting that, to some degree, their own inexperience as educators rendered them powerless to work for change or oppose policies. Daphne, for example, believed that her approach to supporting her students would ultimately prove more effective than the one outlined in the scripted curriculum. Having to follow a prescriptive program which limits her ability to utilize her localized knowledge of students was an aspect of her position that she found deeply frustrating:

> I am really bored teaching a scripted curriculum for eight hours a day. I'm really bored and I'm so frustrated because I have built these relationships with these kids, I love them, I know what they need and I can't give it to them. I'm frustrated beyond belief because I know something that would be better for them but I can't do it.

Other corps members reported a similar disdain for the curriculum but also noted a sense of relief at having a tangible tool at their disposal, even if they considered it an imperfect one. One corps member, for example, in discussing the curriculum he was required to use, said the following:

> Well, if it's going to work then it's kind of like magic—they do it and learn it. If it does not work, it is not my fault and the curriculum failed. If I put myself in it and really commit to making the changes that I think are necessary to make it fit my kids and their needs, it is much more my fault if, at the end of the year, they have not learned anything or haven't progressed.

Although this corps member, like Daphne, expressed convictions about making modifications to certain materials in order to support students, he worried about the sense of responsibility that accompanied such a task. Again, the issue of blame emerged as corps members wondered who or what would be held responsible at the end of the school year if students were unable to make significant academic gains. Moreover, because popular educational rhetoric asserts that scientifically based or research-based curricula, especially in reading, can and does work for all children regardless of background, geographic location or cultural context, modifying or abandoning curricular programs becomes even more challenging (Cochran-Smith & Lytle, 2006).

Fueling this dynamic were corps members' feelings of inadequacy. For example, in an excerpt from a class discussion on the role of the curriculum, Micah expressed his feelings of inadequacy as a practitioner and his resulting decision to privilege the curriculum. Specifically, he likened any deviation from the curriculum to gambling with the futures of his students:

> Micah: Literally I'm looking at this and we can say what we want about the research-based curriculum but those people, most of them have experience before in the classroom and they've gone on to do their PhDs or whatever.

> Instructor: Mostly what people? The ones who wrote the curriculum?

> Micah: Yeah, but I'm saying I can come in and act like I know everything that's going on with the students and I know what's going to work for them because I've known them for a while and I'm gaining something between them. How am I going to know and how am I going to experiment with their future? . . . If I fail, then I'm basically gambling their future on something I don't have the research behind. It's my thinking behind it and I don't have experience in this field so I can't act like I'm the expert when I'm not.

At one point in this excerpt, Micah mentions not having the research to support his instructional moves. This comment suggests that, for Micah, locally generated knowledge does not count as research on which one might base curricular or pedagogical decisions. The discussion Micah and I engaged in is, in many ways, indicative of some of the broader purposes of the course. For example, I hoped that by encouraging students to question the origin of curricular resources and ponder the political motivations behind their adoption by school districts and charter networks, they would adopt a "critically literate" stance within the classroom. As Morrell (2008) notes, "Becoming critically literate entails coming to understand ourselves separately from the discourses that surround us; becoming critically literate also entails having the skills and sensibilities to ask demanding questions of the ideas, concepts and ideologies that are presented to us as fact" (p. 38). Erica spoke to some of the broader implications of these ideas and recognized that while it may seem that teachers are the knowledge holders in the classroom, the authors of the curricular texts play a far more intensive role in determining the kinds of teaching and learning which take place in the classroom. In the excerpt below, she suggested that an overreliance on prescriptive materials implies that teachers do not have the capacity to produce worthwhile knowledge *in practice*:

> I think you're right about what you're saying—if you can make this so that anyone can do it, then you don't really have to worry about making teachers who actually do hold knowledge. We feel like it's a teacher-centered classroom and we're the knowledge holders but we're not really the knowledge holders. Our books are. And we're giving them that knowledge from the book. And I feel really kind of bad saying this, but one of my colleagues recently—I mentioned the curriculum from your charter school and I was like, "You know, they're even talking about the Civil Rights movement and they did stuff around apartheid—" and she was just like, "What's apartheid?" And I was like, "God, you're teaching these kids social studies." There's something about—you don't really have to know your content. You don't have to know anything to teach the content. You do need to know things to manage a classroom. You do . . . and to hopefully adjust the content. But the way that we're structured right now, you just have to hold a book.

Although one of the goals of the course itself was to emphasize the vast, locally situated knowledge that the TFA corps members possessed and to reposition them as critically literate and knowledgeable practitioners, most continued to defer to the curriculum, believing that the curriculum creators knew much more than they did and should be trusted even when aspects of a particular program seemed suspect or remote from the lived experiences of the students. Jason's comments below are typical of this phenomenon; even when he considered a certain activity to be "pointless," he expressed a commitment to stay faithful to curricular mandates:

> There's the question of, "If you're not going to stay faithful, how do you know what it is that you do use and what you don't use?" That's a hard judgment because there are some things where I'm like, "This doesn't make sense. This is pointless." But then there's probably real justification to why it's in there and there are certain skills that I'm not teaching my students because I don't know how.

Interestingly, though many corps members craved the opportunity to create and design aspects of their curriculum, when given the opportunity to create an original unit as one of the methods course assignments, many found that without explicit guidance the task proved unwieldy and daunting. Even when relying almost entirely upon a curricular program to guide instruction, Deneah acknowledged the complexity of making modifications based on what she perceived as her limited knowledge of teaching and learning. Using the metaphor of assembling equipment to explain her frustrations, Deneah felt ill equipped to make the necessary adjustments to her curriculum:

> Even with last week, I was literally sitting there like, "How do I teach them numbers? What is a number? How do you say to a five-year-old this is what a number is? This is what it means to count." So I find that I struggle with that even with my other curriculums because I have to sit there and basically pull everything apart and write out what my kids need and pick and pull and it's like, "Do I need this?" It's like putting together some type of equipment or something but I don't really have all of the pieces that I need.

Like Deneah, Barbara expressed conflicting feelings about the provision of prescriptive materials. Her initial image regarding the kind of knowledge that a reading teacher should possess included the ability to create a comprehensive classroom library and to bring one's experiences to bear on literacy instruction. Instead, Barbara was informed by Excel before the start of the school year that she would be provided with a highly scripted curriculum so she wouldn't "mess up too much":

> I was having a really hard time figuring out what they expected of me as a reading teacher, because I was like, "Oh, reading teacher, so I need to focus on my classroom library and developing my skills in teaching literacy." They were like, "Oh no, you're teaching Reading Mastery. We're going to make sure that you don't mess up too much." At first, I was like, "What?" I was floored. Some small part of me was relieved that they were going to give me this package that would tell me what to do and then on the other hand, this means that I am not injecting any of me or any of what I think reading is into what I teach my kids.

Even though these kinds of sentiments contribute to the deprofessonalization of teachers, Barbara admitted feeling relieved that she would have a tool to rely upon even if it meant her own contributions to literacy instruction would be largely ignored.

Although a number of corps members cited similar feelings of relief in relation to mandated curriculum use, it was evident that being positioned as unknowledgeable practitioners and discouraged from questioning curricular choices exacted a personal toll on both teachers and students. As previously noted in this study, as workers find themselves increasingly replaced by mechanisms of efficiency and utility, they inevitably become alienated from their work (Kliebard, 1975). For example, in discussing what he viewed as an overreliance on the curriculum, one corps member wrote, "This has made me lose confidence in my own ability to think critically and help these students. This has made me think I don't know better or I don't know what to do." Moreover, the alienation that corps members experienced often extended to their relationships with both parents and students. As Caroline explained, she struggled to make curricular justifications to students and their families since she could not always articulate the rationale behind an academic task. In this instance she cited her lack of knowledge about teaching as the reason she was unable to "own" the kinds of learning that occurred in her classroom:

> So in terms of owning my curriculum, honestly this is kind of embarrassing to say, a parent might come up to me and say, "What does my child need to know at the end of first grade?" And I'm like, "Well, you know there are these great things called [state] standards, and I could tell you what he needs to know in the next six weeks because that's as far as my curriculum is going right now." But I've never worked in a way like that before so I think it's a lack of knowledge, and maybe that's my fault, but I've spent the extra time connecting all of the standards of my curriculum, but I don't really own it because I don't really understand the way they thought of it. A lot of times, I don't think my kids know what they're doing.

As Caroline noted here, her own isolation from the reasoning behind the curriculum meant that her students were similarly left with little understanding of the justification underlying classroom activities, a positioning which undoubtedly impedes rather than enhances student learning. Beth had parallel concerns, noting that while TFA Institute was meant to serve as the primary site of preparation for entering the classroom, the use of a scripted program during Institute meant that many of the corps members never had the opportunity to learn how to write lesson plans—an omission which Beth believed added to her overall feelings of inadequacy:

> So we don't really know that this [research-based curriculum] works necessarily in every situation. I feel the same way. I feel like I need to do this as well as I can because I don't know what else to do and I think that's part of the nature of being a Teacher For America, like we don't know what to do. We don't know how to be teachers and what are we doing during Institute? Those of us who taught elementary school, we also taught a scripted curriculum. Some of us have never written lesson plans.

As mentioned previously, because of the abbreviated nature of TFA Institute and the explicit focus on skills acquisition, corps members did not have the opportunity to wrestle with the complexities of teaching. The feelings of inadequacy expressed by Beth are echoed throughout the data by numerous corps members, all of whom felt unprepared and underqualified in their classroom positions. Micah expressed his deference to the curriculum creators who he assumed have PhDs in education and relevant classroom teaching experience. Although he was personally connected to his students, he did not yet feel competent enough as a teacher to make decisions that would alter their academic experience:

> I'm going to be honest with you. I'm underqualified for the position I'm in. There is no doubt about it. I feel like I see other teachers come in and do other things I see in other classrooms and people are just doing a hell of a lot better. I can't keep trying to go off the curriculum and act like this is going to work out if I've never even given the curriculum an actual shot. If there is research behind it and they may have their PhDs, but most of the people who have built it up, they have had teaching experience in the field and they have built it up in a certain way, so I don't feel like I'm strong enough to make those types of comments.

Echoing Micah's assertions, Eleanor noted similar feelings regarding the knowledge which she brought into her classroom teaching experience. She insisted that the only tools she had to draw upon were her personal experience, a curricular guide and whatever experience she could glean from the teacher down the hall. For Eleanor, like Micah, these resources were not sufficient tools from which to build a rigorous learning experience for her students. Further, while she had a sense that something was missing from her instruction and curriculum, she was unsure how or where to locate the information that she needed, leaving her with the sense that she was fundamentally failing her students:

> I was just going to go over what Micah said and I feel the same thing. I feel so underqualified for this that I feel like I have this curriculum and sometimes I think back to first grade and I think, "How did I learn to read?" It worked because I can read now. That's the knowledge I came into this with. I came into this with a book and my own personal experience and then whatever I can pluck from the other teacher who is in her third year of teaching first grade at the school. Those are my three sources of knowledge I come into this with. So it's hard for me to tell myself that I do know something because I feel incredibly underqualified and I am not getting it and not getting what the kids need to get. Where do I find that? I can ask and I can search, but, "How do I get that?"

The majority of corps members, like Eleanor, expressed feeling constrained by the curriculum and noted a commensurate desire to have the freedom to better address the needs of their students.

Knowledge of Students and Culturally Relevant Pedagogy

The methods courses I taught provided an opportunity for teachers to introduce culturally relevant pedagogy into their classrooms as a way both to acknowledge and to embrace the lived experiences of their primarily African American and Latino students. Culturally relevant pedagogy suggests a different conception of knowledge than other instructional philosophies. According to Fox and Gay (1995), "Teachers who practice culturally responsive pedagogy view knowledge as something that is continuously being constructed, recreated, recycled, refined, and re-interpreted" (p. 78). This perspective distinctly contrasts with the mainstream conception of knowledge embodied in most curricular programs. Like the "knowledge-of-practice" conception of teacher learning, advocates of culturally relevant teaching seek to question and problematize mainstream perspectives and dominant narratives.

While my students readily accepted these broader tenets of culturally relevant teaching, the prospect of classroom implementation remained daunting. In attempting to define culturally relevant teaching in more tangible terms, Ladson-Billings (1995) states that within a framework of culturally relevant pedagogy, students must achieve academically, develop a critical consciousness and maintain a sense of cultural competence. The socialization of most TFA corps members divorces academic achievement from both critical consciousness and cultural competence—two elements which I attempted to include in my methods courses. For example, students were asked to design a unit plan which was situated in the local lived realities of the students but which simultaneously aimed to address macro-level systems including immigration, industry, welfare, poverty and racism. A number of students explored neighborhood trajectories, paying careful attention to Ridgeville's transition from a manufacturing economy to a service economy and its resulting impact on the community. As we began designing and sharing curricular projects with one another, we drew upon Banks's (1998) typology of approaches to multicultural education in an effort to unpack what a truly "transformative approach" to culturally relevant instruction might look like (p. 38). According to Banks, both the "contributions approach" and the "ethnic additive approach," which superficially seek to include the experiences of marginalized groups into curriculum and instruction (and are common in mainstream textbooks and prescriptive reading programs), reify stereotypes and trivialize cultures (pp. 37–38). As teachers become more comfortable including multiple perspectives in their teaching and introducing non-Western viewpoints, they will move towards a transformative approach that foregrounds minority perspectives and emphasizes a more complex and nuanced view of historical processes.

While countless corps members expressed a desire during class discussions to pursue this kind of teaching, many continued to feel ill equipped or hesitant to do so. By continuing to read theoretical texts which outlined the philosophical underpinnings of a culturally relevant approach to instruction (Ladson-Billings, 2005; Heath, 1983; Willis, 1995) as well as rich teacher-research accounts which portrayed the intricacies of classroom practice (Bomer & Bomer, 2001; Campano, 2007; Gatto, 2007), we collectively considered how these approaches might be implemented on a daily basis and tried to collectively imagine classrooms that embraced the experiences of all students. Still, many corps members felt hampered not only by the rigidity of their environments but also by concerns that they were not knowledgeable or qualified enough to build and execute curricula based on student experience. Joey, for example, noted the following with regards to his desire to integrate student experience into his classroom:

> This leads me to the biggest question that I came away from this reading with, which is: How do I, as a first-year teacher, integrate students' experiences and stories into my classroom without being singled out for not adhering to the instructional model at my school? Especially in terms of being a Teach For America teacher, I was never trained to use a method of teaching that breaks away from this structure. Furthermore, I've never seen a successful lesson that integrates student experiences or moves away from rote work.

Joey was not only wary of being reprimanded for deviating from school protocol, but he also had no image for what this kind of learning could look like in classrooms. Teachers, according to Fox and Gay (1995), need to "experience culturally responsive teaching from a variety of vantage points, including within their own professional programs of studies, in K–12 classrooms, and in the form of their own attempts under the tutelage of supervisors" (p. 75). Siena, an African American corps member who was eager to provide her fourth-grade students with a more culturally relevant classroom experience than she had had herself, still expressed concerns about how best to introduce such content and methodology: "I have never participated in a class in which students' cultures and histories were given much emphasis, so therefore am really unsure how to begin." Although not from a minority background herself, Dierdre was tasked with teaching a course specifically designed for English Language Learners, many of whom had recently immigrated to Ridgeville from a range of diverse locations. Eager to build upon these deep cultural and geographic histories, Dierdre sought to design an English-learning program that respected the unique and varied stories of her students. However, as a result of her own inexperience as well as the strict administrative mandates enforced by her school, Dierdre felt "powerless" to foreground student stories within the curriculum:

> And all of my students' backgrounds are dramatically different from my own and they possess stories that need to be told and illuminated. I value these stories and I understand the importance in discovering them. However, in many cases I have felt powerless to bring them to light.

Like Joey, Eleanor lamented the lack of images available for this kind of teaching. While she was able to implement some aspects of a culturally relevant approach, like introducing texts that prominently feature African American characters, the more transformative possibilities suggested by a multicultural mindset, like empowering students through curricular design and instructional planning, remained inaccessible to her:

> I know that education needs to be culturally relevant for students and I haven't decided how exactly that looks in my classroom, but I know if I do read-alouds, I get my books from the public library and I pull all African American books mostly so that they see themselves in books. In social studies, we've done some different stuff with African American leaders rather than following the curriculum. I feel like the students should be empowered in their education to make their own decisions and have choice in what they think they need to learn and what they think is beneficial to them, but that's something I don't know how to make possible because I've never seen it modeled or anything.

Although many corps members contended that the dual factors of their own limited knowledge of teaching and the rigidity of their environments confounded their efforts to make learning more meaningful for their students, other teachers considered it their responsibility to "own" their inexperience and, along with it, the prescriptive curricula forced upon them. Some corps members did not experience anxiety regarding use of prescriptive curricula and were able to fulfill their duties without an excessive amount of internal conflict. Jason, for example, rejected the contention that his lack of experience rendered him powerless in the face of school or district administration and, instead, purported that logic and reason could be effectively employed to convince supervisors to make political and structural changes:

> I think with everything, our job is then to own it. So we need to say, "This doesn't make sense." Talk to your administrators and say, "I don't understand this or I don't like this part. To me, it makes more sense to do this." None of those curriculums I think were created for us to blindly follow them and I don't think that's the expectation. I know when it's been given to me, I was never expected to blindly follow. But it's one thing to just change it without talking to administration or something, but if you're worried about someone coming in and seeing that you're not doing that, tell them ahead of time. If you give them the logic, I mean, we're teachers. We went to college and we're intelligent people. They know that they didn't hire us to be babysitters. Just be teachers, so teach.

Daphne offered similar advice to her classmates during a class discussion focused on curricular authority. Daphne's understanding was that corps members were selected by Teach For America, at least in part, due to their penchant for innovation and creativity. In other words, Daphne believed that TFA considers corps members to be problem-solvers above all else, and thus insisted that she possess an institutional mandate to fix those aspects of her instruction which were not advancing the needs of her students.

> For me, absolutely stop and do not give up because you *do* know these kids and you *do* know this material. So what if we didn't have an education background. There's a reason you are here and there's a reason you were picked and you *do* know. A big part of it is our instincts and a big reason we were picked is because we're the kind of people who will be like, "That doesn't work. I'm going to do something different. What am I going to do? I don't know but I'll figure it out and something will come out of my mouth tomorrow." If it works, I'm going to keep going. If it doesn't, I'll do something different tomorrow. We *do* know what's going on and we *do* know how to fix it. No, I don't know everything about Reading Mastery or how it works and maybe I'm missing some pieces because I leave stuff out, but my kids are learning stuff and I can tell you that. They are moving up grade levels, like F and P scores. You *do* know and you are the best one to do it for your kids and I just wanted to say that.

Further, Daphne gauged her relative success, like many of the corps members, according to what she called F and P scores or her students' guided reading levels (Fountas & Pinnell, 2001). Whether she felt like a knowledgeable professional is less important than her students' performance on specific measures of achievement. Daphne's narrative raises questions about what kinds of knowledge fundamentally matter in classrooms and what counts as learning for students and teachers.

Images of Classroom Knowledge and Practice

Many corps members expressed the sentiment that student learning should aim for deep and meaningful engagement with texts and ideas and thus experienced dissonance when forced to promote a style of learning focused on the production and reproduction of rote knowledge. Corps members overwhelmingly expressed, for example, a feeling that students could not express the rationale or justification behind their learning. One corps member, in particular, noted the sense of ennui that can result when work lacks deeper meaning: "When an assignment is done only for one teacher's eyes or for a grade, it is easy to lose track of the 'why' and 'what's the point.' Every student should be able to feel like their work matters." Some corps members chose to address this tension by reminding students of the long-term benefits of academic achievement by mentioning either college entry or career success as a justification for curricular and pedagogical approaches that produced isolation and alienation:

> I have kids every day who say, "Why do we have to learn phonics?" Because we want to learn to read. "Why do we have to learn to read?" So we can do things we want to do. So it turns into this whole thing like, "Well, what do you want to be when you grow up? Everything you could possibly want to be when you grow up, you need to read some stuff to get there. Even if you want to work at a gas station, you need to be able to read things to give people their money back and the forms and everything." So then the kids are like, "Oh, I want to read." The first-graders would say, "I want to read so I can do anything I want." So I feel like kids constantly bring up those questions and always bring up those big goals.

Although students repeatedly sought rationales for classroom learning, this corps member believed that reminding students of broader, overarching goals was productive in instilling a sense of efficacy and agency. Other corps members noted a change in student motivation during times of increased curricular and pedagogical freedom. For example, Barbara and Daphne discussed the change they noticed in the students' dispositions during "Read across America Day":

Barbara: Every one of the kids made Dr. Seuss hats.

Daphne: With word families written on them.

Barbara: And all the kids were like, "Look at my hat." They could explain everything because it was fun and age appropriate and they were learning words. "And we read this book and this is what happened first." I heard kindergarteners sequencing stuff just because they were excited.

Daphne: Yeah, and not because we had this objective. I get that a lot of kids who come in behind, but I don't think that's an excuse to stifle them from being creative, acting their age and doing things that they need to do. It's okay if they color sometimes. They need to color.

Read across America Day, and the alternate purposes for reading which it allowed students to experience, enabled Barbara and Daphne to experience what happens when knowledge is created by rather than transmitted to students. Yet both corps members readily acknowledged that these special events were notable exceptions and that while they were both pleased by the resulting student engagement in literacy, neither felt able to apply these approaches to their everyday classroom activities, which remained largely controlled by the scripted reading program.

Like Barbara and Daphne, Tanya was disappointed by the limited images of knowledge and learning offered to her second-grade students. She noted the sense of alienation which both she and her students experienced in attempting to respect school mandates:

So I think about these kids and I wonder if this is how the whole rebellion begins, like literally hating the institute and hating feeling like I'm becoming a robot and walking the same little line with all the lunch bags and lesson plan books. And in the same format here are the kids walking in little straight lines and coming into my classroom the same way and I'm going to teach them for fifteen minutes and it's all going to go like that.

However, unlike many corps members, Tanya actively resisted this narrow intellectual positioning by abandoning her social studies script and inventing a curriculum that purposefully addressed her students' questions:

And I think social studies has been a pleasure because I just kind of stopped teaching it the way—like my kids were asking about 9/11, and they show a little stupid video of Martin Luther King and how he got separated from the other people, but asking who the other people were. And I saw the video for the first time as I was teaching it to them and I got so irritated that I just started up a whole other lesson about what America was. And it's probably way too much for what they should have learned at age seven years old, but they loved it and I loved it. And we started talking about, well, who killed

Martin Luther King, because we're talking about assassination and sacrifice, and stuff I shouldn't be talking to a seven-year-old. But I think they learned.

Though she noted her students' increased engagement in learning activities, Tanya remained unsure whether these instructional moves were actually appropriate, worrying that class discussions about assassination and sacrifice were too sophisticated for her second-grade students. While most corps members were aware of the limitations related to the transmission model of teaching, they were unlikely to deviate from it without the collective support of a community of teachers with similar intellectual concerns.

Conclusion

Although Teach For America corps members are often lauded for their elite educations, sharp intellects and leadership capabilities, few in this study felt that they could draw upon these resources in the interest of solving problems within their schools and classrooms. In contrast, many doubted the integrity of their knowledge and deferred, instead, to curricular texts and outside experts when making instructional decisions. Although the majority of corps members were forced to use prescriptive teaching materials in their schools and classrooms, many expressed significant dissonance in doing so and voiced a commensurate desire to experiment with more innovative and student-centered practices.

However, when provided with the opportunity through the methods course to actively experiment with curriculum and pedagogy, most corps members were hesitant to significantly alter their practice or to actively resist administrative demands and expectations. For example, while corps members were eager to conduct literacy interviews with their students, some revealed, in doing so, an assumption that quantitative measures functioned as the only legitimate means of assessing students' abilities and planning an instructional program. This in and of itself suggests that a "knowledge-for-practice" framework is not sufficient for the preparation of new teachers, though it is still favored as the primary mode of teacher training, especially in alternative pathway programs like Teach For America in which preparation time is limited. While I tried to make the methods course a space in which teachers could begin to view themselves as knowledgeable practitioners and critically literate individuals, I argue that these spaces must exist across the institutional settings in which corps members find themselves if the goal is to encourage meaningful and long-term practice.

Like Cochran-Smith and Lytle (1999), I hope that by foregrounding the narratives of these teachers I will invite different understandings of what it means to "know" and thus suggest alternate possibilities for school reform. Because an increasing number of educators are being prepared through alternative pathway programs, it is important to consider how these programs situate knowledge and to invite new teachers to consider alternate frameworks. When outside knowledge is consistently privileged, the agency of teachers and students is compromised. Moreover, the work itself, which is at the heart of classroom learning, becomes divorced from meaning, alienating students, teachers and families from the schooling process.

Chapter 6

"A HAPPIER, MORE ENGAGED TEACHER": THE TRANSFORMATIVE POTENTIAL OF THE METHODS CLASSROOM

The previous chapter, documenting the experiences of TFA corps members working in Ridgeville, is incomplete without explicitly attending to the content and pedagogy of the methods courses I taught, which were broadly based on my own theory of transformative practice. Therefore, this chapter details the rationale behind the design of the courses and illustrates how my ongoing efforts to problematize knowledge, foster inquiry and resist the dissemination of "foolproof" strategies provoked tension among the corps members who, at times, had other expectations. While I both highlight and theorize these points of tension, I also share the "moments of possibility" which emerged as a result of the opportunities provided within the course and the kinds of relationships I fostered with a number of corps members. In particular, I discuss how course assignments, readings and discussions led corps members to new understandings of themselves and their students and how these alternate conceptions resulted in the use of alternative pedagogical approaches like collaborative inquiry and culturally relevant teaching.

In addition, this chapter also explores the methods course as a genre, paying particular attention to how methods courses have functioned historically as spaces to transmit a set of technical skills about teaching. In imagining my methods course for first-year TFA corps members, I attempted to disrupt mainstream assumptions about what it means to learn to teach within an alternative pathway program like Teach For America. Moreover, I drew upon the work of innovative teacher educators (Rodgers, 2006; Simon, 2009; Wilson, 1994) to introduce a format for shared inquiry which explicitly invited corps members to critique curriculum, generate classroom-based knowledge and design learning experiences aimed at promoting critical and reflective thinking among students. Many corps members were open to the alternative perspectives put forth in the course and discovered that collaborating closely with peers, drawing on local community knowledge and critiquing and re-envisioning mainstream curricular resources could positively affect their relationships with their students and their overall sense of efficacy as urban educators. Despite the possibilities for meaningful practice suggested by these course experiences, I also theorize the troublesome aspects of my instructional approach, including problematic desires to both empower corps members and re-claim my own experiences as an elementary classroom teacher. Ultimately I argue that only by fostering an atmosphere of shared inquiry within teacher education courses can we collectively prepare new teachers to name, contend with and resist dehumanizing policy mandates that compromise their potential as long-term educators as well as the life chances of their students.

Methods Instruction: Moving towards a Humanizing Pedagogy

Lilia Bartolomé (1994) theorizes some of the problems historically inherent in the "methods" genre. She connects the technical aspects of methods courses, for example, to the underlying and ongoing belief that students' academic deficiencies exist outside of their sociocultural context and thus must be remedied through a series of discrete steps and procedures:

> The solution to the problem of academic underachievement tends to be constructed in primarily methodological and mechanistic terms dislodged from the sociocultural reality that shapes it. That is, the solution to the current underachievement of students from subordinated cultures is often reduced to finding the "right" teaching methods, strategies and pre-packaged curricula that will work with students who do not respond to so-called regular or normal instruction. (p. 174)

Thus, according to Bartolomé, assumptions about students can affect the philosophical underpinnings of methods courses. Teach For America's accelerated timeline for teacher preparation and relentless pursuit of substantial testing gains among students has led to a model of teacher education that predominantly utilizes a transmission model. Corps members, for example, were taught to use one approach to lesson planning and execution, what they called—"the I do, we do, you do" framework—though substantive modes of learning fall outside of this model. Zeichner (1993) refers to this approach as the "social efficiency" model for teacher education and contends that it both emerged from "a faith in science" and can be characterized by the belief that teaching can be reduced to a set of observable and quantifiable tasks. Like Zeichner (1993), Cochran-Smith and Lytle (1993) have critiqued a "social efficiency" approach to teacher education, suggesting that methods courses have traditionally furthered the conception of knowledge as a transferrable commodity capable of being passed from teacher educators to their pre-service and in-service teachers and from those teachers to their students—a stance which positions both teachers and students as passive recipients rather than active creators of knowledge.

Despite this grim depiction, countless teacher educators over the years have sought to re-imagine methods courses as spaces which encourage both innovation and criticality. Simon (2009), for example, who taught a secondary-level English methods course at the University of Pennsylvania, viewed the course as an opportunity to "encourage student teachers to critically interrogate the social and political contexts in which they work, to consider the cultural and linguistic resources their students bring to class and to view their classrooms—and our classroom—as sites of collaborative inquiry" (p. 276). Certainly this stance on methods deviates from the site of technical skills acquisition which Bartolomé describes by inviting students to explicitly contend with the macro-level forces which shape their daily realities as educators. In a similar attempt to interrupt pervasive viewpoints on the genre, Wilson (1994) attempts to broaden her own conception of "method" by introducing alternate perspectives on the term:

> I would have been a better teacher to my earliest students if someone had bothered to teach me that the "methods" required in teaching are multiple: Teachers need to know how to instruct; how to identify, explore and solve pedagogical problems; how to inquire into and learn from their experience; and how to act in ways respectful and moral. (p. 16)

While Wilson's students were initially suspicious of her approach, expecting and perhaps hoping for a more traditional methods experience, many left her classroom with newfound respect for the moral and intellectual complexities of teaching. These re-conceptualizations of the methods genre suggest a deep, underlying commitment to the professional capacities of young teachers. This approach closely aligns with what Zeichner (1993) referred to as a social reconstructionist tradition or "one which emphasizes teachers' abilities to see the social and political implications of their actions and to assess their actions and the social contexts in which they are carried out for their contribution to greater justice, equality, and more humane conditions in schooling and society" (p. 7).

A methods course premised on this definition of teaching must do more than introduce and replicate mainstream practices. It must serve as a platform from which teachers can examine, critique and re-imagine their practice.

Although seldom mentioned in the current discourse on teacher preparation, one of the most radical and "transformative" teacher education programs was developed in the 1950s at the Putney Graduate School in Vermont. In an effort to reject the technical approach to teacher training largely favored at the time, Putney used the term "teacher education" to index not only great skill but also the development of "great love and great awareness" (Rodgers, 2006, p. 1267). In many ways, the vision that Putney's founder, Morris Mitchell (1898–1976), tried to bring to fruition resonates with my own philosophy regarding the purpose of methods courses.

In designing a dynamic teacher education program, Mitchell sought to 1) build upon the knowledge and experiences which pre-service teachers brought to the classroom; 2) disrupt notions of a universal, one-size-fits-all approach to education; 3) design learning experiences which include "inquiring into the social and political structures that both support and deny access to power and opportunity within society"; and 4) thus conceptualize teacher education as "a political problem" (Rodgers, 2006, p. 1269).

Despite the promise inherent in these innovative approaches, the pervasive model of teacher education, particularly within alternative pathway programs like Teach For America, continues to promote methods courses as a site of skill acquisition. As a result, students often enter these courses expecting to acquire a set of strategies which can be effectively implemented across a range of contexts. As Bartolomé (1994) notes, "Although my students are well-intentioned individuals who sincerely wish to create positive learning environments for culturally and linguistically subordinated students, they arrive with the expectation that I will provide them with easy answers in the form of specific instructional methods" (p. 174). Such expectations were undoubtedly at play in my own classroom in which corps members were overwhelmed by their circumstances, confounded by their lack of formal experience and preparation and concerned about student behavior. As a result, they anticipated that my course would provide a set of concrete tools which could easily be transferred from one instructional context to the next. While I was aware of their expectations, I had a competing desire to do something different with the methods course and to help corps members to consider that "learning to teach means entering into critical dialogue—with other teachers, with competing notions of expertise, with the individuals and politics that define and legislate teaching and learning, and most importantly with students" (Simon, 2009, pp. 290–291).

In preparing pre-service teachers, one of Bartolomé's (1994) main aims was to enable her students to move from an object to a subject position, which was one of my sincere hopes for my students as well. I continually sought to create pedagogical and curricular experiences that would position them as agents with knowledge who could make informed and nuanced instructional decisions. I sought to do this by helping corps members to adopt a critical stance towards the materials, methods and curricula they were being asked to implement by Teach For America, Excel and the school district. As Bartolomé (1994) notes, the aim of adopting a critical stance is not the wholesale rejection of any and all methods but rather an informed consideration of why some approaches and curricula might be privileged over others. In addition to analyzing the curricular resources endemic to their schools, the district and TFA, I also explicitly invited students to incorporate the life experiences of their students into the methods classroom as a means of humanizing the methods course and a way to recognize how infrequently the lived experiences of students from marginalized communities are incorporated into classrooms. According to Freire (1970), for example, the kind of banking education pervasive in methods courses functions as a form of dehumanization for both teachers and students. If teachers are not positioned as agents within their pre-service and in-service experiences, it is unlikely they will position their own students as intellectuals capable of sharing knowledge, shaping experience or generating theories and ideas. I hoped to interrupt this paradigm by repeatedly incorporating the lived experiences of students into the methods classroom through readings, assignments and class discussions.

The "Hidden Curriculum": Disrupting Cultural Normativity and Promoting the Re-Professionalization of Teaching

My first encounter with the corps members occurred before the school year actually began during what the university called "Bridge Week"—an initiative aimed at easing the transition between the Teach For America Summer Institute and certification coursework. The weeklong program primarily focused upon building communities of learners and initiating conversations about issues of race/culture within classroom and school settings. While these themes resonated closely with the goals of my courses, the methods instructors, who conducted one-day workshops at the end of Bridge Week, were informed that Bridge

Week was an opportunity to provide concrete, instructional strategies which might be put to use during the first days of the school year.

Although I aimed both to attend to the overarching theme of Bridge Week and to introduce helpful strategies, this initial encounter with corps members resulted in substantial dissonance which continued throughout the semester and served to highlight our different orientations to and expectations for methods instruction. For example, when I asked corps members to share their questions regarding literacy instruction during the Bridge Week experience, nearly all of the questions focused on the "technical" aspects of literacy teaching and learning including an emphasis on decoding skills like blending, segmenting and letter-sound correspondence, suggesting that their preparation during TFA Summer Institute framed literacy as a discrete set of acquirable skills. Other students shared how their own experiences as learners subjected to a "whole language" approach to literacy instruction had handicapped them as teachers. The syllabus I eventually created for the course focused on interrupting conceptions of literacy as an autonomous skill set which could be easily transferred from one context to another (Street, 1984) and sought to problematize popular definitions of literacy which had been promulgated by the National Reading Panel Report (2000) and other media and government venues on which TFA relied.

In addition, my persistence in incorporating the voices of elementary school students and their families into the classroom was an attempt to counter a culture of white, middle-class normativity which first emerged during our Bridge Week discussions and continued throughout the semester. Thus, in all aspects of my teaching—from the course design to the readings to the types of instructional approaches I chose to model for students—I aimed to disrupt cultural norms and encourage teachers to consider the blind spots inherent in their own racial, cultural, political and economic backgrounds and histories. Some of the texts that I selected to use in the course depicted the ways in which mainstream literacy instruction and curricula silence the lived experiences of minority students (Heath, 1983; Willis, 1995). Other readings focused on the experiences of minority students as literacy learners and aimed to illustrate how efforts to build curriculum and pedagogy from student experience proved promising in increasing student engagement and achievement (Campano, 2007; Sleeter, 2005). I consciously selected narratives written by urban classroom teachers in the hopes that the corps members would identify images of possibility in the texts and bring these models to bear on their own classrooms.

In planning the course initially, I was aware that most, though not all, corps members were outsiders with regards to the communities they were entering. Yet even corps members like Alex, who came from marginalized communities, struggled not only with their own preparedness in entering Ridgeville schools but also with the relative preparedness of their more affluent white peers who may have possessed some fundamental misunderstandings regarding urban communities:

> I think it also creates a situation where you get a bunch of highly motivated, affluent people thinking, "Yeah, I can walk into an urban school and teach. That's no problem at all." Of course this is highly problematic. Sure, I went to a really good high school and a really good college and I had a really good job lined up after graduation, but because my parents are immigrants and my parents are not rich, I felt like I could sort of relate to my students and I spoke Spanish, so I felt like less of an outsider coming in. . . . But on the surface when you get a bunch of affluent white people going into predominantly black and Hispanic schools telling them what they have to learn and how they have to learn it, it seems like there are way too many opportunities for conflicts or misunderstandings. Again, TFA has really good talking points about how to deal with those situations. This is very complex. Is it bad to get affluent white people involved in these schools? I guess it's not a bad idea. Perhaps we need more mixing like that.

While Alex did not condemn the potential inherent in outside intervention in urban communities, he struggled to envision how students and teachers who don't share the same background might take up the challenges of diversity. Moreover, even though he shared aspects of his students' background—namely, their language and the experience of having immigrant parents—he still questioned his own assumptions. Other corps members adopted a less critical stance and at times seemed unaware of the ways in which their own backgrounds were affecting their pedagogical and curricular decisions. As part of a course assignment which required corps members to plan and teach a unique literacy lesson, Wendy led her fourth-grade students in a brainstorming session in which they generated a list of books that had been turned into films:

> My students loved generating a list of books and movies. I think the topic may have been what drove their excitement, but they definitely loved seeing me write down all of their suggestions. The list was poor at best—very few of the examples were actual literary works. I think this may come from their lack of exposure to classic children's literature. Instead, they are indoctrinated by pop culture—Samantha's suggestion epitomizes this. She excitedly added Justin Bieber to our list, not just because she loves him, but because "it's a book and they're making a movie!" I had to explain that while a book

and a movie might exist, both are based on his life and are not the types of books and movies we are discussing. Despite this, I put his name on our growing list.

Although students seemed to enjoy the experience and, according to Wendy, were more engaged than usual, she was disturbed by the prevalence of connections to popular culture and assumed their lack of exposure to what she called "classic" children's literature impeded their ability to generate a more comprehensive list of texts. The "classic" texts to which Wendy referred are presumably those which she read and appreciated during her own childhood. Moreover, although familiarity with popular culture suggests a certain level of media literacy, Wendy did not view this as an asset.

As Popkewitz (1998) notes, these unexamined frameworks of normativity are problematic in those settings in which teachers are attempting to work across lines of difference: "Within this space the best these children can hope for is to become like the normal person. Thus teachers disciplined children's attitudes and emotions so that they learned to renounce a set of populational characteristics ascribed to them as personal psychological characteristics" (p. 68). In a separate assignment in the literacy course, Wendy struggled again to separate the experiences of her students from her own experiences, once again applying her own normative lens as a middle-class, white teacher to the everyday family activities her students participated in:

> I guess the Shirley Bryce Heath article really hit me about different literacy at home, so I asked a lot of questions that I thought could help me categorize them. I asked if they could identify a newspaper and if they could name any sort of newspaper. I also asked if they could name a magazine. They couldn't. I also thought about ways my parents had incorporated literacy into my life as a kid and one of the things I kept coming back to is whenever we would go anywhere in the car, we would look at signs and look at license plates, letters and patterns. I asked them what they do in a long car ride. None of them look out the window. They are all playing their Nintendo DS, their PSP, sleeping, listening to music.

In Wendy's assessment of Heath's (1983) landmark text and how it relates to the experiences of her students, she focused almost entirely on literacy content. For example, in asking her students about the kinds of texts they read at home or the kinds of activities they engaged in while riding in the car, Wendy was viewing literacy primarily as a set of skills or activities that we acquire rather than something that we put to use in our interactions with others. Zipin (2009) recounts a similar phenomenon with regards to classroom "funds of knowledge." According to Zipin, "As cultural learning resources, *ways of knowing and transacting knowledge* cut deeper than knowledge *contents*, in that they are not only embedded in locales but embedded 'in' people, as deep, more-or-less subconscious dispositions" (p. 325, emphasis in original). In other words, Zipin recognizes that countless meaningful pedagogical interactions occur among students and their families and communities outside of school, though these are not often formally recognized as "funds of knowledge" within classroom contexts. Although through course readings I aimed to introduce a perspective on literacy which sought to emphasize the wide range of experiences students might draw upon in classroom communications, including the ability to use analogies, engage in sophisticated analysis or suggest and defend a point of view, Wendy struggled to move beyond her belief that literacy ability is commensurate with knowledge of literacy content. As Popkewitz (1998) further asserts, "In other situations, discourses of teaching focused on the classroom as a place where the weaknesses/deficiencies of children's upbringing could be overcome. The classroom was a place to transmit 'wholesome, caring values and traditional ethics'" (p. 67). Similarly, course assignments meant to build upon student experience were sometimes taken up as opportunities to remediate assumed student, family and community deficiencies. By continuing to frame students' experiences in light of their own upbringings, corps members struggled to recognize value in child-rearing practices and cultural beliefs which differed from their own. A specific aim of the course was to have open discussions about topics like racism, white privilege and poverty, as these issues would often surface in written course assignments but were seldom explicitly addressed during course discussions.

The Methods Course as Shared Inquiry

In addition to introducing course texts with the objective of explicitly disrupting mainstream literacy paradigms, I also reconfigured the design of the course with the hopes that instead of foregrounding skills acquisition I would emphasize a multicultural approach to the teaching of reading and writing which allowed space for a range of voices. As a researcher situated within the paradigm of critical, collaborative feminist research, one of my hopes was to help participants think beyond the immediacy of their current experience as classroom teachers in Ridgeville (LeCompte, 1994). In an effort to transcend the urgency of the everyday in which corps members often sought quick fixes to classroom issues, I framed the course as a shared inquiry and de-centered myself as the primary knower and disseminator of knowledge. Like many educators who spend the majority of their day alone with children, corps members were placed in school settings in which they primarily taught in isolation and thus were hesitant about sharing their work with one another.

To counter this tendency, I sought to create collaborative spaces. Students in my class were placed in inquiry groups for the duration of the semester. They met in these groups on a weekly basis to discuss readings or to share their writing. One of the tenets of the course was that all coursework was shared publicly either in a whole-class discussion or among the small inquiry group in an effort to de-mystify classroom practice. Drawing upon Gitlin and Thompson (1995), I hoped to establish an environment in which "the conditions for conversation as method are set in place such that 'we' relationships can develop . . . [and so that] the teacher, the learner and the knowledge produced are inseparable" (p. 145).

And yet, creating a classroom atmosphere which emphasized the collective rather than the individual was not always easy. As Weiler (1991) notes, "Feminist pedagogy within the academic classrooms addresses heterogeneous groups of students within a competitive and individualistic culture in which the teacher holds institutional power and responsibility (even though she may want to reject that power)" (p. 129). Corps members repeatedly noted that the collaborative nature of the course was unique and could not be found either within their schools or within TFA. As one corps member stated:

> I looked forward to our discussions. It was rough. We were all in crazy places, but it was something I looked forward to. TFA didn't really provide that kind of thing. Even though it was a formal class, it still felt informal. It felt like a support group in a way or a discussion group or a teacher cooperative and the TFA events, when we did get together, were more just like business. It was like. "this is mandatory and you won't get your AmeriCorps award."

Many corps members made analogies to support groups when theorizing the kinds of intellectual collaboration which took place in the classroom, a sentiment that resonates with feminist discourses which position feeling, emotion and intuition as valid ways of knowing (Bernal, 1998). Drawing on Audre Lorde, Weiler (1991) notes the following,

> Lorde's discussion of feeling and the erotic as a source of power and knowledge is based on the assumption that human beings have the capacity to feel and know and can engage in self-critique; people are not completely shaped by dominant discourse. (p. 135)

The regular inquiry group meetings and discussions not only served as spaces of self-critique for corps members as they wrestled with challenging aspects of their classroom practice but also became informal sites of resistance to dominant discourses of teaching and learning. As teachers designed their own, locally contextualized curriculum, they relied heavily on insights from their inquiry group as they wrestled with how to approach administrators, create space for alternative practices and otherwise negotiate district mandates in order to implement the curriculum they created.

Caroline, another corps member, used the metaphor of the support network to comment on a different aspect of the course. Specifically, she was concerned with the course requirement that all coursework be shared publicly, an instructional decision designed to deepen the sense of interdependence among corps members. According to Caroline, the support she received in her small inquiry community made the more public aspects of the assignments less intimidating:

> I think the way it's been structured from the beginning is kind of neat. It wasn't, "Write a lesson and here are these people you haven't been in communication with to essentially rate how good it is." It was more like, "You're going to go through the process with two other individuals." So we started the brainstorming process in this group of three and then kind of continued it. I don't care about posting my stuff but I would imagine that would make somebody feel slightly more comfortable because they've kind of had this support network, if you want to call it that, throughout the entire process.

For Caroline, the fact that groups collaborated across space and time helped to mediate the risk and uncertainty she might have felt in making her teaching public. Annika expressed a similar sentiment, noting in particular that the kind of feedback she received from her small inquiry community transcended categories like "good" and "bad," to which she had become accustomed in terms of evaluation. Moreover, the work which took place within the inquiry community was not merely for show. Rather, she received feedback that was actually useful and began to value collaboration in new ways:

> I think one thing I really enjoyed this year is collaboration with other teachers because my school doesn't really foster that at all, and we read each other's lesson plans as we team plan but no one ever says, "That was a good idea or that was a bad idea or why didn't you try that?" It was helpful just to not be blowing in the wind not knowing what I'm doing with someone reading this. I felt like they really read it and really gave

me feedback and it might actually be better because of it. That's so not been a part of my year so it was nice to have that.

Further, corps members noticed when a sense of sharing and community were emphasized in other settings as well. For example, in another university course which aimed to explore race, culture and urban education, Katrina noted the kind of rapport which was established through group discussions and the kind of support she received from both the professor and her peers:

> It was very much like a support group because there were people in that class from a wide spectrum of experiences and beliefs about our communities. Even so, I had moments where I was really angry and wanted to get up and punch people, but it was like a community where I actually felt like I'm learning and they're learning but they may not come to meet me where I'm at by the end of this class, but they're learning as teachers. [The professor] always said, "You need to deal with your own shit." They were learning how to do that. I thought that was really valuable. I felt like they should make all of the first years take that.

As noted previously, educational change requires collaboration; it is necessary, then, for teachers to work together in the interest of resisting prescriptive curricula and punitive environments for children. In their research, for example, Achinstein and Ogawa (2006) specifically note the necessity of community in furthering an agenda of change. As the authors state, "Their resistance could not be sustained alone; rather they needed to be supported by a strong community that reinforced their alternative perspectives and continuous questioning of the dominant messages" (p. 58).

In spite of some of the positive ways in which the course functioned for certain participants, many expressed frustration and tension regarding my explicit decision to de-center myself as the primary knower in the classroom. Corps members shared concerns regarding whether they were receiving enough concrete strategies from the course itself and sometimes adopted a doubting stance towards the practices I did explicitly model, which suggested that their students could (or should) work collaboratively, write silently or share openly in response to texts. The corps members voiced the majority of these frustrations via weekly note cards which they submitted at the end of class as a means of providing feedback. I referred to the cards as "gots/needs" cards and asked them to record not only what they gleaned from a particular class session but also what they thought they still needed moving forward. I then used the cards as a means for planning future classes or responding individually to the needs of particular students. The resistance of the students to the course content resonates with Orner's (1992) provocative question regarding agendas of empowerment: "How can we understand 'resistance' by students to education which is designed to empower them?" (p. 75). While I was convinced that if students took a believing stance towards the course and chose to embrace collaboration, creativity and intellectual rigor, they might see a difference in their classrooms, I struggled with their complaints and unhappiness and possessed an equally strong desire to facilitate a course that they found useful and practical. Thus, I also offered a litany of concrete tools and strategies for teaching reading, writing and social studies content which teachers could incorporate alongside their scripted curricular programs. While many corps members likely did find these useful, I discovered that transformative practice occurred only when corps members embraced alternative approaches. For example, when corps members truly drew upon the experiences of their students in designing curriculum and relied upon student-centered practices as the primary means for instruction, they not only saw their students differently but began to view themselves differently as well.

Shifting Views of Students

The reflections which corps members were required to complete after teaching the lessons and units that they designed are rife with examples of how experimenting with pedagogy allowed for a more expansive view of student knowledge and ability. In constructing the rationales for the lessons and units that they designed in the course, corps members expressed an eagerness to try new approaches in the hopes that doing so would encourage student investment. Deneah noted, for example, that her kindergarten students reported that they hated school as a result of the kinds of rote learning enforced at such a young age:

> Each student in my small group proceeded to tell me how hard school was and how the routine of completing worksheets does not change. Some of my students even went as far to say that they hated school because they never get to do something they enjoy.

Similarly, in designing his lesson, Joey sought to deviate from the mandated instructional model he employed most days in an effort to see how his students would respond. Like many corps members who viewed these assignments as opportunities to experiment with different approaches to learning, Joey discovered that his students were more engaged and motivated when they felt some ownership over the lesson content:

This lesson was certainly different from the more cut-and-dry, systematic lessons I teach. While this one did not strongly follow the [Excel] direct instructional model, I felt that it was much more developmentally appropriate for students, and also allowed them to be creative and become engaged in something that they were able to produce on their own.

In addition to discovering an increased level of student engagement, corps members found that their students thrived when allowed to participate in alternative instructional formats, like group work, which the corps members had previously considered untenable. Joey, for example, who taught social studies to third- and fifth-grade students in a highly tracked environment which emphasized individual achievement over collaboration, was curious about how his students would respond to cooperative learning. In experimenting with a more collaborative approach, Joey discovered that his students actually could function productively in groups—an outcome he hadn't expected:

At [Excel], there is very little time for students to ever socialize outside of lunch, and so it was very informative to see that my students actually could function in groups self-contained and run by students. Students were engaged working with their peers and many felt driven by the tasks set for each group, and even students who I often see slouching or disengaged from work were giving their input and pushing the group along. Even the quiet students were cheering for their own group after they got up to present and also clapping loudly for their fellow classmates. And when I told the class at the beginning that we were going to be working on a group project that day, I'm not sure, but I think I heard a few unexpected gasps and a few quiet cheers. I think in this sense, it was a wonderful breath of fresh air for both myself and the students to break out of the ordinary and produce some work that allowed for a melding of ideas and information.

Joey referred to the opportunity to try something different as a "breath of fresh air," a metaphor that suggests how stifling the highly scripted classroom can feel to both students and teachers. Moreover, while Joey believed that students' unfamiliarity with group work and collaboration would make introducing such protocols challenging, he found the opposite to be true, discovering that those students who were typically disengaged during traditional lessons became eager participants when given the opportunity to work with peers. Beth, a fifth-grade teacher, also chose to experiment with group work as part of her lesson plan assignment and wrote the following:

A variety of elements in this lesson went very well, particularly group work and reading aloud. Normally, when I assign group work for my students, it is very difficult to keep them on task, even when I monitor them closely. In this case, however, the students were actively engaged in the materials. They did not discuss weekend plans or pass notes. Instead, they listened to each other read and discuss the story. Rather than having to re-explain the directions seven times because that many students were not paying attention, I spent my time monitoring student progress. For once, everyone was paying attention! The read-aloud element also went particularly well. The students directed themselves, and took turns around their circles. Because I chose stories at their independent levels, most students felt comfortable reading out loud. If one of the students did not want to read, the other students encouraged them to read but did not push them. Even my "lowest" students were actively engaged and did their best work.

Like Joey, Beth found that students could not only "handle" more interactive participation structures like group work and read-aloud but in doing so, they also exceeded her expectations. Experimenting with content and pedagogy in this way allowed Beth to view even her "lowest" students from a platform of possibility and to consider that a more expansive instructional repertoire might be necessary in order to reach them effectively.

While Brooke, like her peers, was eager to introduce cooperative learning into her classroom, in reflecting upon her use of group work during her unit plan assignment she realized that her students were accustomed to viewing her as the primary source of knowledge within the classroom and thus their ability to work effectively with one another was compromised:

> In practice, my students functioned well in groups but were unaccustomed to being so responsible for their own readings and their own ability to contribute to discussion without my leading them. My students still see me as the bearer of knowledge, and making the transition to get them to see their peers as capable of discerning knowledge from articles was tricky.

Brooke insightfully noted that varying instructional practice cannot be a one-time occurrence if longer-term change is the ultimate goal. Students become accustomed to thinking and acting in particular ways and interrupting such patterns once is not enough to promote the kind of lasting transformation that many corps members hoped for. Cecily encountered a similar problem; by experimenting with new instructional approaches she realized how reliant her students had become on the kinds of rigid instruction which she had used to guide her teaching for the bulk of the school year:

> I realize that I, as a teacher, enabled this problem throughout the year. Because I leaned so heavily on concrete assignments with very clear, black-or-white style answers, my students had a hard time beginning to construct knowledge. . . . Rather than make

guesses, they expressed helplessness. I predict that I can remedy this with my students next year by forcing them to engage in more discovery-style learning. I need to help students realize how much they may already know before providing them with all of the answers. That uncomfortable feeling of searching for answers amidst uncertainty will create initiative taking, critically thinking students instead of multiple-choice answer selectors. Changing the dynamic that the students must be completely dependent on me for new knowledge will also help me shift the ownership over learning in the classroom to my students. These are all goals I have not only for teaching this unit again in the future, but also for teaching my future classes in all subjects, generally.

Reflecting on her own practice through the teaching of the lesson allowed Cecily to realize that that she had, unknowingly perhaps, been in the process of preparing students to become expert test-takers rather than the critical thinkers she hoped to inspire. Seeing her students struggle with uncertainty was a reminder to Cecily that she needed to provide more opportunities for them to engage with real questions and problems in the hopes that by doing so they would become more comfortable with nuance and complexity.

Experimenting with instruction not only allowed corps members to view their students through a lens of possibility but also encouraged them to reflect critically on the kinds of practices that had been privileged in their classrooms previously. For example, engaging with students differently allowed Joey to reconsider his own understandings of what constitutes learning. In the following excerpt, Joey critiqued his school's overreliance on quizzes and tests, in part because he worried that they ultimately serve to undermine both teacher and student investment:

One of my large goals for this project was for students to create something of value to themselves and to me. I have felt recently that I've been moving along the school year with my students taking in information, and then outputting it in the form of quizzes and tests. The students are not excited to complete worksheets and quizzes, and I am not excited to grade them. Therefore, I wanted to create a task for students to be creative and become invested in the work that they were producing.

In a parallel kind of reflection, Amelia traced how her understanding of what constitutes true learning had evolved as the result of teaching a unit about the war in Iraq. Concerned that her fourth-grade students had oversimplified notions regarding the war and struggled to truly embrace a stance other than their own, Amelia designed a unit which aimed to introduce the students to many of the complex issues surrounding the 2003 invasion of Iraq and the war that followed. In considering what the students had learned, Amelia wrote the following:

> In their final reflections on the unit, when asked to write freely of their feelings regarding this particular war, and war generally, many students declined from taking sides. In an informed indecisiveness unusual for their age, they thoughtfully considered evidence, opinion and ethics. They produced writing which many might accuse of being sloppy and poorly argued because they attempted to inhabit so many stances within one page. I consider these confused writings successes exemplary of their thoughts. I know my students can argue a side—they did so wonderfully in our three-day debate. But I am happy to see their dichotomous ethical systems shaken, if only a little.

Although Amelia conceded that outsiders might view their writing as sloppy or disorganized, she recognized that her students had grown in their ability to consider the complexity inherent in a particular situation. Amelia's discoveries about teaching paralleled, in many ways, her students' discoveries about the war in Iraq, In particular, experimenting with pedagogy and content allowed Amelia to reconsider what counts as teaching and learning. Corps members who assumed that their students would struggle to work collaboratively in groups or who doubted the capabilities of particular students were surprised when they embraced assignments or materials enthusiastically. In Amelia's case, the unit assignment allowed her to gain a deeper understanding of and appreciation for Iliana, whom she describes as one of her most difficult students:

> Iliana, arguably my most difficult fourth-grader, wrote three opening statements for her team for homework (unprompted by me). At the bottom of the page, she included guiding questions that sound like mine when I teach (Why do you think that? Can you tell a little more about that?) Presumably she planned on encouraging her teammates in this way. Iliana's opening statement is certainly not the most well-written, but the effort and the ideas expressed in it were huge for her. I am embarrassed to admit how surprised I was to see her excel. She also wrote a research paper at home (which I had not assigned). During the debate, she made sure everyone on her team was informed of the arguments and had something to contribute (this is a student who has had extreme challenges getting along with others). No miracles occurred, but I watched otherwise reluctant students wake up. I, in turn, became a happier, more engaged teacher.

Again, a student who had previously been viewed as obstinate and uncooperative was able to re-invent herself through the alternate pedagogies and curricula which Amelia introduced. But Iliana was not the only one transformed in the process. In recognizing her students' assets and capabilities, Amelia, like Joey, felt happier and more engaged in the classroom. In a final reflection on the outcomes of her unit, Amelia confessed her anxiety prior to beginning the unit and considered the promising outcomes:

> I have also learned that I have held my students to low expectations. I had no idea until I realized how surprised I was to see them learning, and enjoying it. I was worried about this unit. I did not think my students would be interested, and I thought the complexity would be too challenging. My students were absolutely challenged and, as I said, are still a little confused about the facts. But when I prompted my students to write about what they learned this year, the majority wrote about the war in Iraq.

While these examples suggest that new teachers should have the opportunity to experiment with pedagogical and curricular approaches within a supportive professional community, too often TFA corps members are trained in only one or two instructional approaches. When these prove alienating or ineffective, teachers seldom have recourse to improve the learning experiences of their students. Moreover, as corps members encounter repeated failure in the classroom, their own sense of efficacy is diminished. Assignments like the ones described above not only allow corps members to reconsider their views of students, they also encourage them to adopt identities as knowledgeable and informed practitioners capable of creating classrooms that are inviting and engaging spaces.

Shifting Views of Self

As corps members experimented with pedagogy and curriculum through course assignments, some of them began to adopt a critical stance on their classroom teaching and to recognize and analyze potentially problematic practices. Throughout the course itself, Tanya had been an outspoken critic of many of her school's values, including tracking, rote instruction and what she viewed as the de-professionalization of teachers. However, after having the opportunity to teach a literacy lesson which she designed, Tanya began to recognize the ways in which she contributed to some of the very practices she sought to interrupt. For example, though she attempted to problematize and eradicate tracking within her school, in teaching her lesson and allowing her students to work in cooperative groups, she realized that the students had internalized her conceptions of them as high- or low-achieving students:

> I also took note of the one Yellow group member that came into a place of power as secretary. I heard a student say, "I pick her because she writes well." I wondered to myself, when had they ever seen her writing? But then I remembered, I had paid her a

very large compliment during class for writing so neatly and clearly. I found this interesting because it made me wonder if I had complimented members of Red group enough publically. I often pay compliments to my students while in their leveled groups but the majority of my public compliments are usually directed towards Green and Yellow group (Red group tends to have the most behavioral issues and therefore has less opportunities to be complimented).

If students had not been invited to collaborate in groups during this lesson, Tanya might not have realized the ways in which students were both interpreting and applying the categories to which they had been assigned. In a similar kind of reflection, Wendy considered the ways in which she had been limiting the voices of her students by selectively highlighting some of their answers during brainstorming sessions:

> While I normally call on students to participate, this was one of the first times I allowed ALL of their suggestions to make it to the board. In an effort to keep my lessons on track, I usually modify my students' suggestions or politely reword their ideas. In doing the opposite—and putting all suggestions on the board—I validated my students and their knowledge. . . . This lesson (and its successes) is going to encourage me to identify more ways and opportunities to draw upon my students' knowledge and experiences. They need to have a greater participatory role in class—which will increase their engagement.

As a teacher who had repeatedly struggled with student engagement, Wendy used the lesson as an opportunity to experiment with ways to modify and increase student participation. Without a specific invitation to think and act differently, Wendy, like Tanya, might not have been able to critically reflect upon the troubling aspects of her practice.

While most teachers were eager for the opportunities to experiment that the lesson and unit plan assignments afforded, many were also fearful of retribution from the school or district. However, in actually enacting lessons that deviated from school or district expectations, numerous teachers discovered that their fears were actually unfounded. Annika, for example, who taught her unit in the final few weeks of the school year, realized that her refusal to deviate from her mandated script was based more on unsubstantiated fear rather than actual action taken by her administration:

> In the final weeks of the school year, I finally realized my belief that excitement in learning arises from learning in the field. In retrospect, the only reason that I did not act sooner was an unsubstantiated fear that my administration would disapprove of such rich learning experiences. In addition, I lacked the confidence in myself as a teach-

er to successfully engage and follow through with a city-as-classroom learning expedition. By letting go of my own inhibitions as a teacher, I finally gave my students a chance to learn in an authentic and engaging manner.

Moreover, by reconnecting with her own deeply held beliefs about education, Annika was able to create the kind of classroom she hoped to design from the start. Although Annika believed deeply that the city itself could serve as a meaningful laboratory for learning, at the start of the school year, she lacked the confidence and perhaps encouragement to act on these convictions and get her students out of the building and into the surrounding community. Nadine similarly recognized that her classroom was lacking uncertainty, an element that Nadine considered essential for learning. Like Annika, Nadine implied that her uncritical adherence to the rigid instruction model made it difficult to re-imagine her classroom:

> That confusion, however, is exactly what was missing from my classroom. Confusion and uncertainty and curiosity drive learning in young people, and I was depriving them of that process of discovery and meaning building because I was adhering to a rigid direct instruction model. By modeling student interactions for my class, closing out lessons with whole group reflection and giving students creative outlets to display their learning, I became more comfortable facilitating engaging student-driven lessons. Their level of engagement increased automatically. They all felt like experts of sorts because they instantly had a degree of knowledge about [their town] and were entertained by the anecdotal history they devoured through texts, movie clips, pictures and interviews.

However, once Nadine decided to deviate from the curricular and pedagogical approaches to which she had become accustomed, she realized that she possessed the potential to position both her students (and herself) as experts capable of producing important community-based knowledge. As Copenhaver-Johnson (2007) notes, "Anyone familiar with classroom-based research conducted in culturally diverse classroom settings recognizes that cultural responsiveness cannot be prepackaged in a list of 'what works' in classrooms" (p. 44).

Finally, although Cecily had an image of herself as a student-centered teacher, she recognized that this identity was largely dormant due to the demands of her situation. Thus she considered the unit plan assignment an opportunity to re-invent herself as an educator:

> These were the feelings and reflections I had experienced by the time I began teaching my social studies unit. I hoped that the unit would give me a chance to practice being the teacher that I philosophically wanted to be. I wrote the unit with my desire to take advantage of an opportunity to practice being a more student-centered teacher at heart.

Although many corps members entered the teaching profession having had limited experience with students, curriculum or pedagogy, many still held deep convictions regarding the kinds of educators they hoped to be and the kinds of practices they sought to draw upon. The course, then, provided a supportive venue through which teachers could consider, enact and reflect upon their long-held convictions about teaching and learning. In addition to enacting her vision of transformative education the way that Nadine and Annika had, Annette also viewed the results of her unit assignment as valuable data which supported her convictions that teaching approaches should be multiple and varied and reflective of the needs of students in a particular context:

> It was also very different to depart from a scripted curriculum for my content area. I follow along every day and am given standards that I must teach. There is a pacing guide that I must stick to because administrators could walk into my classroom at any moment. I drill the students with facts that they need to memorize during each class period. It was refreshing that I finally got a chance to form what I thought the students needed and were missing in my curriculum. I gathered all of the materials for the lesson, created it from scratch and took pride in what I had developed. Although it was a more creative lesson, where students could be imaginative and artistic, I still kept in mind district learning standards and explored the topic in different ways. This lesson just confirmed my belief that all mandated texts are not the best.

Annette demonstrated that a more student-centered or creative approach to teaching is not synonymous with the abandonment of district standards or other guidelines which have been generated by policy makers. Rather, the two can coexist when new teachers have the support and guidance to explore different approaches and the freedom to experiment with approaches which they believe will better meet the needs of their particular students.

Although for many corps members these assignments served as an incentive to alter their daily classroom practice, adopt different teacher identities and draw upon both their local contexts and their convictions about teaching and learning, for some, the administrative constraints endemic to their schools proved too powerful. Edith, a corps member deeply committed to social justice and student-centered teaching, found that she could not teach the afterschool unit she originally designed due in part to concerns regarding student achievement and pressure from her administration to make sure that all of her third-grade students were reading on grade level by the end of the school year:

> The suggestion from my administration came coupled with my own urgency to finish helping my remaining four students to read on grade level. And so began the siphoning

off of my original intentions; and in its place appeared a class too similar to what I'd created in my scripted classroom. It was April and I was tired of fighting the directives and my curriculum. Also, I knew that the year was in its last months and that I still had students who needed to master the basic skill of reading. And so, in the space I had specifically created to liberate myself and my students from basic-skills curriculum, I couldn't help but feel the pressure to let my original ideas hit the sidelines. Each week I came prepared to do my lesson and community-oriented activity, but I would watch the clock eat away minutes as I pushed sight words and extended individual reading time to work independently with my group of struggling readers.

Although Edith, like most corps members, had a strong desire to ground her curriculum in the lived experiences of her students and to draw upon community resources, she was both fatigued by the pressure to conform to the constant directives of her administrators and concerned that if she abandoned basic-skills instruction, then her students would not attain grade-level proficiency in reading. Thus, her desire to imagine a different kind of classroom, no matter how strong, did not overrule her belief that skills instruction is more important or, at least, must exist apart from more open-ended kinds of instruction. Moreover, despite my efforts within the course to broaden definitions of literacy instruction and question paradigms which equate literacy with skills, Edith still equated remedial reading with a "skill and drill" approach to instruction and did not believe that the social justice unit she designed would adequately address the skills and abilities her students were lacking. Edith's resistance to broader definitions of literacy could be due, in part, to the materials disseminated by TFA during the Summer Institute in which literacy is specifically framed as an autonomous set of skills (Street, 1984). In answer to the question, "What is literacy?" the document lists the following components: "book and print awareness, phonemic and phonological awareness, phonics and the alphabetic principle, word and structural analysis, reading fluency, reading comprehension strategies, writing skills and strategies" (p. 19). While the authors advocate for a balanced literacy approach, which they define as a union between decoding and comprehension strategies, the guidebook clearly favors phonics. This kind of framework invites little conversation regarding what good literacy instruction could look like and how it might vary according to context. Thus, TFA teachers have little opportunity to engage in open debate about what qualifies as effective reading and writing instruction. Rather, they are handed a mandate with clear directions about how literacy should be defined and subsequently disseminated.

Pedagogical Possibilities: When Teachers Learn Differently, Students Learn Differently

Aside from the promise and potential suggested by corps members' shifting perspectives with regards to their students and themselves, there was also evidence that when teachers were invited to learn differently as part of their preparation program, students learned differently as well (Cochran-Smith & Lytle, 2006). For example, because the unit plan assignment for social studies methods focused on designing curriculum which was both rooted in the local community and reflective of larger questions, corps members had to seek out community experts; research topics of interest from non-mainstream perspectives; and grapple with broader questions regarding the political, economic and social forces which had shaped Ridgeville. In order to fulfill the requirements of the assignment, corps members had to actively engage with the community and listen to and learn from students, parents and peers. As a result, many corps members created unit plans that invited students to engage in a similar kind of learning. For example, concerned that her students experienced a certain level of dislocation because they attended a charter school far from their respective neighborhoods, Annika designed a unit on city planning which required her students to analyze the original plan for the layout of the city, map their individual neighborhoods and consider the goods and services available in the school neighborhood. Students participated in fieldwork on one of the oldest streets in the country and presented their final maps to peers, parents and community members as an authentic means for demonstrating their learning.

Similarly, because a number of readings in the course focused on disrupting deficit orientations and viewing marginalized students from an asset perspective, Dierdre, an ELL teacher, built a unit around highlighting her students' diverse language abilities and capacities. In recognition that she was required to teach nonfiction reading and writing, Dierdre decided to tie these instructional objectives to the cultural backgrounds of her students by inviting them to write an original autobiography which included personal anecdotes, factual information related to their country of origin and stylistic approaches representative of the genre of autobiography. Dierdre also took her work a step further by inviting the school community and the students' families to view a public exhibition of the work, a move which effectively moved the ELL program from the margins of the school to the center (Gitlin, Buendia, Crosland, & Doumbia, 2003), inspiring other students to inquire about whether they could also join the class.

In addition to attempting to broaden conceptions of literacy through the methods course and offering opportunities for corps members to both design and teach lessons and units which built directly upon the experiences of their students and attempted to speak to their unique cultural histories and narratives, at its most basic level, course assignments offered corps members an opportunity to deviate from the script. Although Caroline, a first-grade teacher, did not choose to use the unit assignment as a chance to delve into aspects of her students' cultural histories, she did recognize the instructional power in temporarily abandoning prescriptive curricula and incorporating student voice into the classroom:

> It was one of the first times that my students were talking about themselves in our classroom. Perhaps for many of them it was the first time they learned about each other. And, everyone was engaged.

Like Wendy and a host of other corps members, Caroline often expressed frustration with student engagement. In allowing students to share openly, however, she found that "everyone was engaged."

Other corps members took the assignment a step further and chose topics for exploration that were meant to reflect the cultural background of their students. Nancy, for example, was concerned that the Black Power movement was either absent from mainstream curricular materials or dismissed as a violent and ineffective arm of the Civil Rights movement. Knowing that the Black Power movement had an important history in Ridgeville, Nancy sought to plan a unit that would help her predominantly African American third-graders comprehend the importance of the Black Power movement in the fight for equal rights. Corps members like Nancy, who used the assignments as a chance to explore culturally relevant teaching, came away from the experience convinced of the importance of basing instruction on students' lived experiences:

> The two and a half weeks that I spent teaching this unit invested me further in the notion that knowledge of self and the history of one's culture can be a truly motivating experience that leads to academic and behavioral success. Because this unit expanded beyond what we did in the classroom, it was a small taste of what culturally competent learning can look like when parents and families are used as funds of knowledge.

More important, the course provided an explicit opportunity for teachers, like Nancy, who were already interested in culturally relevant approaches, to build curriculum within a safe and supportive community environment.

Informed by teacher-research accounts like Campano's (2008) which depict the power of locally driven, student-specific curriculum, Nancy planned to overhaul her entire third-grade social studies curriculum:

> Implementing this Unit Plan in my classroom has further convinced me of the importance of the "second classroom" that Campano discusses, and I am working to create an African American studies curriculum (in lieu of the provided social studies curriculum) for my third-graders next year that encompasses numerous aspects of this unit plan.

Again, this kind of example suggests that asking novice educators to engage in transformative instructional practices or to entirely reconfigure their classroom curriculum may not be a feasible goal, at least initially. However, it does suggest that providing opportunities to experiment with culturally relevant content and pedagogy within a supportive and caring community can provide the impetus teachers like Nancy need to take their work a step further.

Conclusion

In many ways, my journey as a course instructor paralleled the experiences of the corps members as I attempted to figure out what it meant to teach graduate students in a post-secondary context. Essentially, we were all novice educators learning from and with each other through the course. Like the corps members, I sometimes failed to maintain a productive classroom community and experienced tension and disappointment when certain instructional moves did not produce the results that I desired. Moreover, as much as I attempted to discourage the corps members from adopting a deficit view of their students, I felt challenged, at times, to view their assets and capabilities as educators rather than merely to focus upon those areas that concerned me or that I thought needed improvement. In discussing my work with others, I often deferred to collectively describing my students as "TFA teachers," a term which, in certain contexts, indexed a lack of experience, a scripted pedagogical approach and a future trajectory which did not include teaching. The corps members in my course certainly represented a wide variation of experience, preferences and stances and I often had to remind myself to attend to their passions and capacities rather than their insecurities or weaknesses.

Similarly, although one of the main motivations for designing the course was to interrupt the corps members' notions of normativity, I found that I often applied my own framework regarding "best practices" or "good teaching" to the methods classroom and, in many ways, sought to have my students adopt these definitions. When I shared examples from my own fifth-grade classroom, I often did so with the expectation that corps members would view my approaches as instructional models to which they should aspire. Similarly, I sometimes viewed the course as an opportunity to re-live my own elementary teaching experiences and to inspire the corps members to become the kind of teacher that I once was without also problematizing my own practice. While I tried to remain aware of these tendencies and realized they were contrary to the kind of inquiry environment which I hoped to create, I often found it difficult to let go of the notion that there is a "better way" to teach literacy and social studies. Moreover, due to some of my own assumptions about the values of TFA and the school district, I struggled to be open to the ways in which the corps members approached teaching and learning, especially when it contrasted distinctly with my own instructional ideas and approaches. For example, when corps members raved about a test prep strategy that "really worked" or a writing approach that helped students produce formulaic essays, my reaction was sometimes cynical, believing that these classroom victories did not actually count as real learning. As a result of these tendencies, I had to be vigilant about rejecting the "expert" role as a course instructor as in many ways I wanted corps members to readily adopt certain instructional approaches which I deemed "effective."

While I do believe that the course served as a transformative space for many corps members as suggested above and that many of the TFA teachers felt more "empowered" as educators within restrictive institutional settings as a result of our course explorations, I am aware of the problematic dynamics which can result when empowerment is part of the teaching agenda (Ellsworth, 1989). By acting with transparency in regards to my agenda, for example, it was not difficult for corps members to discern my political and philosophical stance with regards to education and thus respond to readings or complete assignments in ways that resonated with my beliefs. As noted previously, for example, I asked a student to revise a paper that was particularly laden with deficit language. Although she willingly completed the revision, I wondered, in retrospect, whether she had learned anything substantive by making the changes or whether she simply determined the stance I considered most appropriate and adopted it.

Another empowerment issue that emerged involved the emphasis placed on student voice in the classroom. Because the course was framed as a collaborative inquiry, and I seldom asserted myself as an "expert" or "knowledge-holder," some uncomfortable moments occurred during class discussions. In one instance, a corps member shared that her African American students did not speak English, implying that their use of a vernacular dialect rendered them linguistically deficient. While I was aware of the necessity to interrupt such thinking, I was also hesitant to directly challenge the student and disrupt the atmosphere of harmony I had managed to cultivate. Like Achinstein (2002), I recognize that conflict is an essential part of community and that communities that actively avoid conflict usually harbor hidden angst and frustration. Yet, as a young teacher educator still learning how to guide adults through discussions of complicated systems like racism and poverty, I often opted to avoid uncomfortable encounters, even with the knowledge that such tactics might ultimately lead to more, rather than less, conflict.

Like the corps members, I was painfully aware of my own inadequacies as an instructor as I worked within and against institutional constraints in order to bring my educational vision to fruition. Ultimately, recognizing and responding to these parallel challenges made me a better professor; through considering them I was able both to acknowledge the complexity of my task and to develop empathy for the corps members who were asked to teach under exceptionally trying circumstances.

Chapter 7

RECONSIDERING THE POSSIBLE IN URBAN EDUCATION: EMBRACING MULTIPLE NARRATIVES

Like many people who return from difficult settings abroad, I struggled to explain my experience in Congo to my friends and family back home. I felt angry that Americans seemed to know little about the war, and so I sought to communicate the scale of the suffering. At the same time, I was afraid that the descriptions of hunger, violence and corruption—very real facets of Congolese life—would reify pervasive images of Africa as a savage, depressing and lawless continent. Thus, when asked about Bukavu, the city where I lived, I almost always emphasized its beauty, purposefully omitting other images and eliding much of the hardship I encountered. Negotiating my narrative about Congo became one of the most difficult aspects of the time that I spent there. Ultimately, I came to believe that there was no right way to talk about central Africa, and so I stopped discussing it at all, subtly shifting topics when someone asked a particularly probing question. I knew there were many stories that needed to be told, yet I often found it easier either to remain silent or to relate the narrative that most people expected to hear—a single story which depicted Congo as one of the most terrible places in the world and denied the nuance, humanity and depth of my experience.

During my tenure as an instructor for Teach For America, I observed the corps members struggling with a similar phenomenon as they embodied a number of different tensions. For example, recruited for their intelligence, creativity and leadership capabilities, corps members often found themselves positioned as low-level workers subject to outside mechanisms of control and unable to alter curriculum in order to meet the needs of their students. As narrators of their experience, these young teachers had to carefully consider how to represent urban schooling to outsiders eager for their assessment of the state of education in the United States. Corps members used these storytelling opportunities as a way to make sense of the inequities they encountered. Many were unprepared for the conditions of Ridgeville and found few institutional spaces which afforded them the opportunity to wrestle with the issues they confronted on a daily basis like racism, poverty and immigration. Moreover, corps members were simultaneously attempting to negotiate their role within the national educational narrative in light of the significant pressure they experienced as individuals tasked with trying to improve the life chances of their students.

As a teacher-researcher, I believed one of my primary responsibilities in working with corps members was to broaden the range of stories available to them regarding students and schooling. By adopting a stance of "possibility," I hoped to interrupt mainstream perceptions of urban environments as fundamentally depraved settings and to invite corps members to view urban teaching as a creative, demanding and rewarding career. While these goals were sometimes met with resistance and the work itself did not always succeed, critical insights offered by the corps members, combined with the transformative learning opportunities which many of them created for their students, suggest important implications for how new teachers come to understand the limitations and possibilities inherent in their teaching contexts and how these understandings engender or hinder their ability to work for lasting educational change.

Findings

Several key findings emerged from the study which have significant implications for the fields of literacy and teacher education. I first detail the most significant findings, then discuss their relevance and finally highlight practical and theoretical implications.

- First, the analytical lenses teachers apply to their practice affect the ways in which they both approach pedagogy and curriculum and negotiate their relationships with students, families and colleagues. While only one corps member in this study used the word "Taylorism" to describe his tenure with Teach For America, numerous corps members implicitly invoked this framework by drawing upon factory terminology to theorize their experiences. By mentioning efficiency, production, assembly lines and strict oversight, corps members revealed the extent of their de-professionalization.

While many corps members were aware of how a lens like Taylorism influenced their beliefs and practices related to schooling, other, less obvious frames were at work in the discourse of the corps members as well. For example, when asked to describe their students, many corps members deferred to a deficit framework that included depictions of students, families and communities as ignorant, violent and dysfunctional. Similarly, when asked about knowledge, corps members consistently privileged the perspectives of curriculum "experts." What is most relevant to this study is that corps members employed the lenses that were both readily available to them and seemingly useful in making sense of their experiences. This suggests that the availability of other, alternative lenses might yield different understandings and different practices in the classroom, an idea that is explored further in the discussion of potential implications.

- A second finding contends that the intertwining contexts of the Ridgeville School District, the Excel Charter Network and Teach For America made the questioning of these lenses particularly challenging. The shared philosophies of these institutions, which promoted a reliance on quantitative measures, narrow definitions of literacy teaching and learning and problematic portrayals of urban students, conspired to make the introduction and application of alternative lenses difficult. Even those corps members who entered TFA with a strong desire to teach in a culturally relevant manner or cultivate deep connections with students, families and communities often ended up abandoning these desires in light of institutional constraints. Thus, while the methods course can introduce and encourage "transformative" approaches to instruction, unless other contexts evolve accordingly, broadening the range of possibilities within urban education remains unlikely.

- A third finding of this study suggests that the methods course can serve as a site of re-professionalization by creating experiences that reconnect teachers to their practice, their students, their colleagues and themselves. The moments of "possibility" experienced by corps members during the methods course occurred, in part, as a result of the deep collaboration that teachers were involved in as they met in inquiry groups to design curriculum, share problems of practice and consider alternative pedagogies. Corps members noted repeatedly how important our shared inquiry was to their emotional, social and intellectual development as teachers. Although the corps members came to Ridgeville as part of a cohort of Teach For America educators dedicated to achieving change in the city, the trainings and professional developments provided by TFA were, according to corps members, focused exclusively on the transmission of "teaching" skills rather than the collaborative generation and creation of knowledge. Prior to entering my courses, many had never publicly shared their lesson plans with anyone. The methods course became one of the few spaces in which corps members were invited to authentically engage with one another. The opportunity, then, to collaborate around meaningful work and to make work public helped teachers to re-position themselves as knowledgeable practitioners capable of making and justifying complex instructional decisions.

- The final finding, which is grounded in the work of Cochran-Smith and Lytle (2006), suggests that "when teachers learn differently, students learn differently" (p. 689). According to Cochran-Smith and Lytle, "When teachers at all levels of experience are encouraged to ask questions, their students are more likely to find themselves in classrooms where their own questions, not rote answers, signal active and consequential engagement with ideas" (pp. 689–690). In other words, methods courses must transcend the current predilection for technical knowledge so that pre-service teachers can engage deeply with alternative pedagogical approaches like shared inquiry, critical pedagogy and culturally relevant teaching. If our goal as teacher educators is to prepare thoughtful and reflective practitioners, then we must design and teach courses that embody these hopes. Numerous teachers, for example, used the course as an opportunity to meaningfully experiment with curriculum and pedagogy by designing units and lessons that drew on community resources and knowledge bases. Other corps members arranged for students to have meaningful experiences outside of the classroom and experimented with participation structures within the classroom that invited and acknowledged alternative ways of being and knowing. Finally, corps members created opportunities for their students to share their work with authentic audiences, which naturally increased engagement among a wider scope of students. Moreover, many corps members, for example, found the collaborative aspects of the course to be particularly useful and, as a result, began to introduce more group work into their classrooms. While these teachers were deeply skeptical about their students' ability to collaborate productively, most corps members discovered that when structured appropriately, these experiences possessed the potential to deepen and enrich student learning. However, despite the emphasis I placed on creating opportunities for teachers to learn differently, many corps members still expressed concerns that they did not feel capable of incorporating culturally relevant or critical pedagogical approaches into their classrooms. While corps members reported seeing value in these approaches and believed their own K–12 experiences would have been enriched by the inclusion of multiple perspectives or an emphasis on criticality, many worried that they did not possess the competencies necessary to effectively introduce and facilitate such approaches with their own students and preferred, instead, to rely upon the curricular resources provided by the school or district.

Discussion

The Teach For America corps members in Ridgeville were situated at the nexus of a number of competing discourses, a positioning which complicated their ability to create and sustain change within classroom, school and community settings. Recruited for their ingenuity and then made to follow rigid mandates, they had to negotiate a range of differing perspectives on how best to attain educational justice for marginalized students. My course provided a site in which many of these discourses overlapped and intersected, thus offering an opportunity to observe and engage with corps members as they wrestled with the challenges of teaching and learning in urban contexts.

Although Teach For America insists that corps members are identified and selected for their ingenuity, creativity and leadership capabilities, the corps members featured in this study were universally positioned as low-level workers and lauded for their adherence to top-down mandates and fidelity to curricular materials. As a result of this "silencing," corps members began to doubt their own abilities and were thus reluctant to try new approaches even when the mandated techniques proved ineffectual. While the most pervasive critiques of TFA have focused on the ways in which corps members are ill equipped to contend with and address issues facing urban students—both academic and social—I argue here that the most critical element of their lack of experience is the way in which it renders them less likely to oppose and question policy mandates that are potentially damaging to them and their students. For example, while corps members readily identified a number of problematic practices within their schools, including tracking at the elementary level, empty rhetoric surrounding college attendance and the reliance on behavior modification techniques to control students, none felt as though they could confidently approach administrators or district personnel to express their concerns. Thus, over the course of the academic year, corps members came to embody the competing discourses which surrounded them.

Because corps members were simultaneously teaching and learning within three distinct institutions, namely, Teach For America, the university and the school district, they had to negotiate each institution's perspective on student achievement and social justice, which often existed in contrast to one another. While the discourse of TFA emphasized student achievement on standardized measures as the primary means for assessing educational attainment, Excel and the school district added a discourse of college attendance and future achievement as potential indicators of success. The university offered a slightly different orientation by emphasizing student empowerment, lifelong learning and authentic inquiry. Interestingly, while these features of the university's program diverged most from corps members' daily experience in urban schools, they featured prominently in corps members' own educational backgrounds and experiences. Thus, while corps members could identify the ways in which they had benefited from open-ended and inclusive instruction, when confronted with the challenge of having to teach across lines of difference in settings in which many perceived students as academically deficient, the corps members tended to rely on the approaches favored by TFA, the school district and Excel rather than on their own philosophical or personal beliefs about learning.

The emphasis on efficiency which many corps members found so troubling in their teaching sites was also a key component in their own preparation as educators. Most of their formal "training," in fact, stands in stark contrast to Lytle's (2006) "literacies of teaching" framework which encourages rich and varied dialogue across constituencies, deep collaborative relationships and the questioning of mainstream perspectives on knowledge. Corps members reported that their TFA preparation framed students, families and communities as deficient, relied on narrow definitions of literacy learning and required that they prepare and teach lessons in isolation with little meaningful input or contact with peers and colleagues. Without the space or opportunity to position themselves as literate practitioners capable of designing and implementing more effective teaching approaches, corps members had little choice but to accept discourses which rendered them ill equipped and incapable.

Accordingly, alternative route programs like TFA offer important insights into the ways in which dominant educational discourses currently function within U.S. society. As schools of education are depicted as obsolete and alternative pathway programs grow in reach and scope, reliance on scripted programs, quick fixes and "best practices" will likely increase, reflecting an oversimplified view of education—one which elides the nuance and complexity of the profession. Teachers who choose to matriculate in alternative pathway programs may begin to internalize the mechanistic views of teaching they once actively resisted and translate these perspectives into careers in other sectors. In other words, if corps members enter positions as policy makers or educational leaders with the belief that teaching involves little more than reading from a script, they are likely to further agendas which de-professionalize and disempower teachers.

Therefore, as the reach and influence of alternative programs continue to expand, providing opportunities for the teachers enrolled in these programs to question and problematize mainstream depictions of teaching and learning becomes ever more critical. Partnerships between schools of education and alternative pathway programs can offer teachers other lenses through which to consider the complexities of urban education. For example, many corps members reported that Teach For America did not emphasize structural or systemic inequality when theorizing student underachievement. This perspective, however, was a key component of the university discourse to which corps members were exposed throughout their certification coursework. Without the opportunity to consider the ways in which U.S. society has systematically prevented poor and minority students from achieving educational and economic success, corps members are left with an overly simplistic narrative which presents social mobility as an easily attainable, unequivocal good premised on the merits of the individual.

Moreover, broader debates focused on the "best" ways to prepare teachers should explicitly include the voices of corps members and other educators who choose to enter teaching through alternative pathway programs. These teachers often possess salient and incisive critiques of their preparation programs that are seldom reported in mainstream media accounts—an omission that significantly limits the depth and range of possible conversations regarding teacher certification. Mainstream debates that depict schools of education as archaic institutions inhibiting educational change and organizations like TFA as crusaders eager to reform corrupt public systems serve only to contribute to ongoing stagnation. Teach For America—and programs like it—are unlikely to disappear. Rather, their reach and influence continue to expand. However, without meaningful partnerships with schools of education and the inclusion of multiple narratives regarding urban student achievement, curriculum and instruction and social mobility, these programs will likely produce teachers who feel disillusioned and overpowered by a system that extols efficiency and compliance at the expense of creativity.

Implications

There are a number of theoretical and practical implications to these findings which make the results of this study particularly relevant to the realms of urban education and teacher preparation.

The Significance of Analytical Lenses

As mentioned above, the conceptual and analytical lenses that the corps members applied to their experiences as urban educators offer important insights into their modes of sense-making and should be attended to by teacher educators and others who support them. The fact that many corps members drew upon Taylorism as the primary lens for situating their experiences in urban schools indicates their pervasive feelings of dehumanization and disempowerment. By creating spaces in which teachers can both acknowledge and analyze the kinds of frameworks they bring to their classrooms, we are inviting them into a tradition of critical practice. In doing so, we can encourage corps members to consider the economic and political forces which influence the everyday operations of schooling and to contend with a discourse of structural and systemic inequality otherwise elided in their preparation by Teach For America. Furthermore, by recognizing these frameworks as a starting point for working with corps members in teacher education courses, we can model what it means to make student knowledge a starting point for classroom instruction. In addition, TFA corps members might benefit from being introduced to alternative frameworks—ones which offer more empowering portrayals of teachers, students and classrooms. While the framework of Taylorism speaks to the context of Ridgeville in an age of particularly severe reform initiatives, it may actually limit what corps members consider to be possible within urban schools more broadly. One of our goals as teacher educators should be to expose new teachers to a range of frameworks that could inform and shape their experiences in urban contexts. In doing so, we might expand their conceptual repertoire and influence their curricular and pedagogical choices. I am not trying to suggest that this is a simple process, as rudimentary introductions to approaches like critical literacy and culturally relevant pedagogy proved inadequate for many corps members who were seeking ways to transform their practice. Moreover, the intense pressure to conform to school district mandates subverted attempts by corps members to experiment with alternative ways of thinking about teaching and learning, a limitation which is challenging to adequately address outside of a policy setting.

Re-Imagining the Methods Classroom

A second implication of this research is the need to reverse the current trend of the de-professionalization of teachers and to frame teachers, instead, as literate individuals who are capable of making informed decisions about curriculum and pedagogy. In order to accomplish this goal, which in many ways directly counters the current narrative about urban teachers, is to reconsider the role of methods courses within alternative teacher preparation programs. Instead of continuing to frame methods courses as primarily a site of skills acquisition, these mandatory courses could be re-imagined as spaces centered on collegiality and collaboration, thus actively de-centering the professor as the primary source of educational knowledge. Not only would pre-service and in-service teachers be viewed as capable practitioners; urban students, families and communities also could be seen as possessing important resources and assets which are applicable and transferable to the classroom.

In terms of content, methods courses associated with and designed by programs like TFA need to move beyond the technical transmission of knowledge and instead situate teacher learning in light of local and national policies as well as historical, social and economic conditions so that new teachers do not view the processes of teaching and learning as isolated from these factors. Too often, methods courses are positioned outside of the more political aspects of schooling and viewed as a neutral zone in which teachers acquire autonomous knowledge that can be indiscriminately applied to multiple contexts. Moreover, issues of equity and diversity are notably absent from the courses that TFA corps members take during their Summer Institute. By divorcing these concerns from the methods courses, however, leaders within TFA are missing an opportunity to unite theory and practice and to demonstrate how macro-level concerns within education are enacted each day in local contexts. By helping new teachers connect their everyday practice with the broader political climate, teacher educators can subvert the de-professionalization of teaching. As novice educators are encouraged to link practice and policy and take stances against dehumanizing policies, the possibility for lasting change becomes possible.

Pedagogies of Possibility

A significant aspect of re-imagining the methods course involves considering how to alter the kinds of pedagogies typically introduced in these contexts. As mentioned above, methods courses have traditionally favored a transmission-style approach to instruction in lieu of focusing on the broader political implications of relying on such pedagogies. This study suggests the value in explicitly incorporating other pedagogical approaches into the methods classroom, including culturally relevant, critical and feminist pedagogies, as these approaches specifically engage political, economic, cultural and social concerns within the realm of education.

The corps members in this study, for example, found that the lived experiences of their students were largely ignored by the mandated curriculum, rendering meaningful instruction impossible. Although corps members could readily recognize the limitations of prescriptive curricular resources, many were hesitant to introduce alternative pedagogies, believing they did not possess the knowledge or skills necessary to do so. It seems, then, that pre-service and in-service teachers would benefit from repeated exposure to these alternative pedagogies as well as explicit invitations to implement them in the classroom. Corps members nearly universally expressed both a strong desire to introduce these pedagogies to their students and a commensurate concern that they did not possess the knowledge and experience necessary to do so. Thus, the brief exposure which my students received to these practices was not sufficient to overcome their feelings of self-doubt. Therefore, I argue that if we want novice educators to embrace alternative pedagogies, we must situate these practices at the heart of our own instruction as teacher educators. Further, those corps members who did attempt to put these approaches into practice experienced promising results with their students. For example, the use of such instructional approaches allowed many corps members to begin to see their students from an asset rather than a deficit orientation—a shift, which in and of itself, has the potential to radically alter both classroom climate and student performance.

Finally, repeated exposure to alternative pedagogies should be woven throughout teacher preparation programs in the hopes that new teachers will have opportunities to experiment with these kinds of approaches in their own elementary classrooms. Moreover, although countless studies support the notion that students from marginalized backgrounds tend to learn better in educational settings which draw upon a range of pedagogies and acknowledge their cultural backgrounds (Phelan, Davidson, & Yu, 1997), corps members needed to see these approaches at work in their own classrooms to be convinced of their potential to positively affect student learning.

Policy, Practice and Activism

Finally, I argue that we must consider how to expand the channels of communication that currently exist among universities, local policy makers and institutions like Teach For America, as relationships between these constituencies critically inform and shape the socialization of new teachers. While leadership within these various institutions made significant attempts to collaborate and deliver a cohesive message to corps members, the teachers in this study struggled to reconcile the divergent viewpoints. As mentioned previously, "Bridge Week," which was held each August, was meant to serve as a philosophical segue between Summer Institute and the certification program at the university. Yet, despite concerted efforts to clarify the role of each organization, misunderstandings persisted as corps members struggled to define the role each institution would play in their growth and learning. Moreover, while the leadership of these institutions did seek to proactively communicate around differences, few institutionally sanctioned spaces existed in which corps members could discuss and problematize the stances they encountered. Thus, many brought these concerns into the methods course and actively wrestled with how to interpret and apply the contrastive philosophies of the institutions to which they belonged. For example, while the university, the district and Teach For America all make claims of working towards social justice for traditionally underserved students, the efforts undertaken to achieve these outcomes varied greatly, depending on the institution. Thus, corps members were quick to recognize that each setting emphasized distinct and sometimes incongruous aspects of teaching and learning. While university courses tended to focus on inquiry, collaboration and student-centered instruction, Teach For America and the district stressed the importance of student test scores as measures of academic success and achievement. Corps members struggled, at times, to simultaneously inhabit each of these spaces as they attempted to refine their own views and beliefs about urban education. As a course instructor affiliated with the university, I tried to create opportunities to discuss openly the dissonance they encountered. However, these kinds of conversations should have taken place across contexts with specific attention to how corps members could practically negotiate the differing expectations and begin to form their own opinions and beliefs regarding urban teaching and learning. Moreover, as national rhetoric around education reform becomes more embittered, it becomes increasingly urgent (and difficult) to provide examples of how productive and generative dialogue can occur across theoretical stances.

Yet, encouraging corps members to constantly question policies and voice concerns about educational approaches might have unforeseen consequences. Many corps members, for example, worried that a direct questioning of curricular and pedagogical practice could compromise their standing among supervisors and colleagues. One of the challenges posed by this study, then, is how to encourage corps members (or novice educators, more generally) to work for change in ways that do not jeopardize their job security. Moreover, it is equally important to consider the ways in which the short tenure required by TFA affects how corps members negotiate the dissonance they experience in urban settings. Believing that they may eventually move on to careers in other sectors can both enhance and limit the kinds of conversations they choose to invest in as classroom teachers. Some may fear that they have nothing to lose by making their beliefs known publicly while others may find the threat of censure and reprimand a sufficient deterrent to speaking up, especially when they do not anticipate pursuing a long-term career in the classroom. Ultimately, it is easier to conform to dehumanizing mandates when these compromises are viewed as short term, a notion which potentially inhibits the kinds of activism in which new teachers might choose to engage.

Conclusion

In his foundational text "The Narrative Construction of Reality," Jerome Bruner (1991) writes that narrative is a form "not only representing reality but of constituting reality" (p. 5). Bruner is claiming, then, that the stories we tell are often the stories we live, a notion which has significant implications for my attempts to understand and theorize the experiences of Teach For America corps members. As these new teachers contended with the daily challenges of urban teaching, they became authors of their experience and composed stories regarding what kinds of teaching and learning were possible in urban contexts. In authoring these "texts," corps members had to rely upon the lenses available to them, however limiting. These lenses not only engendered deficit views of students and families but also compromised the kinds of teaching and learning which corps members imagined to be possible in the Ridgeville schools. When corps members consistently viewed students as being in need of remediation and viewed themselves as incapable of subverting curricular mandates, their educational visions were significantly hindered.

One way to conceptualize teacher education, then, is as a site of authorship. Within their preparation programs and the range of institutional contexts that inform their experiences, teachers should be encouraged to write with and against mainstream narratives of urban schooling and, in so doing, to create new stories that highlight the capacities and potential of students and teachers. In the final line of her novel *Jazz*, Toni Morrison (1992, p. 229) writes, "Say make me, remake me. You are free to do it and I am free to let you because look, look. Look where your hands are. Now." Morrison is playing with the idea of authorship; she is inviting us to question the role of the reader in creating texts. The corps members who choose to dedicate two years of their lives to urban settings would benefit from a similar invitation—one that asks them to author their experience, to imagine alternate realities, to re-shape urban schooling and, in so doing, to change the story.

Bibliography

Achinstein, B. (2002). Conflict amid community: The micropolitics of teacher collaboration. *Teachers College Record, 104*(3), 421–455.

Achinstein, B., & Ogawa, R. (2006). (In)Fidelity: What the resistance of new teachers reveals about professional principles and prescriptive educational policies. *Harvard Educational Review, 76*(1), 30–63.

Adichie, C. (2009, July). *Chimamanda Adichie: The danger of a single story* [Video file]. Retrieved from http://www.ted.com/talks/chimamanda_adichie_the_danger_of_a_single_story.html

Anderson, M. (1998). "You save my life today, but for what tomorrow?" Some moral dilemmas of humanitarian aid. In J. Moore (Ed.), *Hard choices: Moral dilemmas in humanitarian intervention* (pp. 137–156). Lanham, MD: Rowman & Littlefield.

Au, W. (2011). Teaching under the new Taylorism: High-stakes testing and the standardization of the 21st century curriculum. *Journal of Curriculum Studies, 43*(1), 25–45.

Banks, J. (1998). Approaches to multicultural curricular reform. In *Beyond heroes and holidays: A practical guide to K–12 anti-racist, multicultural education and staff development* (pp. 37–38). Washington, DC: Network of Educators of the Americas.

Bartolomé, L. (1994). Beyond the methods fetish: Toward a humanizing pedagogy. *Harvard Educational Review, 64*(2), 173–194.

Bernal, D. (1998). Using a Chicana feminist epistemology in educational research. *Harvard Educational Review, 68*(4), 555–582.

Bomer, R., & Bomer, K. (2001). Writing for social action: Collaborating on texts for public purposes. In *For a better world: Writing for social action* (pp. 122–154). Portsmouth, NH: Heinemann.

Boyd, D., Grossman, P., Lankford, H., Loeb, S., & Wyckoff, J. (2006). How changes in entry requirements alter the teacher workforce and affect student achievement. *Education Finance and Policy, 1*(2), 176–216.

Bruner, J. (1991). The narrative construction of reality. *Critical Inquiry, 18*(1), 1–21.

Buck, P., & Skilton-Sylvester, P. (2005). Preservice teachers enter urban communities: Coupling funds of knowledge research and critical pedagogy in teacher education. In N. González, L. Moll, & C. Amanti (Eds.), *Funds of knowledge: Theorizing practices in households, communities and classrooms* (pp. 213–232). Mahwah, NJ: Lawrence Erlbaum.

Callahan, R. (1962). *Education and the cult of efficiency.* Chicago: University of Chicago Press.

Campano, G. (2007). *Immigrant students and literacy.* New York: Teachers College Press.

Cochran-Smith, M., & Fries, M. K. (2001). Sticks, stones, and ideology: The discourse of reform in teacher education. *Educational Researcher, 30*(8), 3–15.

Cochran-Smith, M., & Lytle, S. (1993). *Inside/outside: Teacher research and knowledge*. New York: Teachers College Press.

Cochran-Smith, M., & Lytle. S. (1999). Relationships of knowledge and practice: Teacher learning in communities. *Review of Research in Education, 24*(1), 249–305.

Cochran-Smith, M., & Lytle, S. (2006). Troubling images of teaching in No Child Left Behind. *Harvard Educational Review, 76*(4), 688–697.

Cochran-Smith, M., & Lytle, S. (2009). *Inquiry as stance*. New York: Teachers College Press.

Copenhaver-Johnson, J. (2007). Rolling back advances in multicultural education: No Child Left Behind and "highly qualified teachers." *Multicultural Perspectives, 9*(4), 40–47.

Creswell, J. (2007). *Qualitative inquiry and research design* (2nd ed.). Thousand Oaks, CA: Sage.

Darling-Hammond, L. (1994). Who will speak for the children? How "Teach For America" hurts urban schools and students. *Phi Delta Kappan, 76*, 21–34.

Darling-Hammond, L., Holtzman, D. J., Gatlin, S. J., & Heilig, J. V. (2005). Does teacher preparation matter? Evidence about teacher certification, Teach For America, and teacher effectiveness. *Education Policy Analysis Archives, 13*(42), 1–50.

Dawes, J. (2007). *That the world may know: Bearing witness to atrocity*. Cambridge, MA: Harvard University Press.

Decker, P. T., Mayer, D. P., & Glazerman, S. (2004). *The effects of Teach For America on students: Findings from a national evaluation*. Princeton, NJ: Mathematica.

Dillon, S. (2009, January 13). Few specifics from education pick. *The New York Times*.

Donaldson, M., & Moore-Johnson, S. (2011, October 4). TFA teachers: How long do they teach? Why do they leave? *Education Week*.

Easterly, W. (2006). *The white man's burden: Why the West's efforts to aid the rest have done so much ill and so little good*. New York: Penguin.

Ellsworth, E. (1989). Why doesn't this feel empowering? Working through the repressive myths of critical pedagogy. *Harvard Educational Review, 59*(3), 297–324.

Fairbanks, A. (2011, July 27). Walton Family Foundation gifts Teach For America 49.5 million. *The Huffington Post*.

Flores, B., Cousin, P., & Diaz, E. (1991). Transforming deficit myths about learning, language, and culture. *Language Arts, 68*(5), 369–379.

Fordham, S. (1999). Dissin' "the standard": Ebonics as guerilla warfare at Capital High. *Anthropology & Education Quarterly, 30*(3), 272–293.

Foucault, M. (1977). *Discipline and punish: The birth of the prison*. New York: Random House.

Fountas, I., & Pinnell, G. (2001). *Guiding readers and writers*. Portsmouth, NH: Heinemann.

Fox, W., & Gay, G. (1995). Integrating multicultural and curriculum principles in teacher education. *Peabody Journal of Education, 70*(3), 64–82.

Freire, P. (1970). *Pedagogy of the oppressed*. New York: Continuum.

Gatto, L. (2007). Success guaranteed literacy programs: I don't buy it! In J. Larson (Ed.), *Literacy as snake oil: Beyond the quick fix* (Rev. ed. 71–88). New York: Peter Lang.

Gee, J. (2000) Identity as an analytic lens for research in education. *Review of Research in Education, 2*, 99–125.

Gibson, M. (2005). Promoting academic engagement among minority youth: Implications from John Ogbu's Shaker Heights ethnography. *International Journal of Qualitative Studies in Education, 19*(5), 581–603.

Gibson, M., & Hidalgo, N. (2009). Bridges to success in high school for migrant youth. *Teachers College Record, 111*(3), 683–711.

Gitlin, A., Buendia, E., Crosland, K., & Doumbia, F. (2003). The production of margin and center: Welcoming-unwelcoming of immigrant students. *American Educational Research Journal, 40*(1), 91–122.

Gitlin, A., & Thompson, A. (1995). Creating spaces for reconstructing knowledge in feminist pedagogy. *Educational Theory, 45*(2), 125–150.

Green, J., & Bloome, D. (1997). Ethnography and ethnographers of and in education: A situated perspective. In J. Flood, S. B. Heath, & D. Lapp (Eds.), *Handbook of research on teaching literacy through the communicative and visual arts* (pp. 181–202). New York: Macmillan.

Hart, B., & Risley, R. T. (1995). *Meaningful differences in the everyday experience of young American children.* Baltimore: Paul H. Brookes.

Heath, S. (1983). *Ways with words: Language, life and work in communities and classrooms.* Cambridge, UK: Cambridge University Press.

Herr, K., & Anderson, G. (2005). *The action research dissertation.* Thousand Oaks, CA: Sage.

Hopkins, M. (2008). Training the next teachers for America: A proposal for reconceptualizing Teach For America. *Phi Delta Kappan, 89*(10), 721–725.

Kagan, D. (1992). Professional growth among pre-service and beginning teachers. *Review of Educational Research, 62*, 129–169.

Kamler, B. (2001). *Relocating the personal.* Albany: State University of New York Press.

Kennedy, D. (2004). *The dark side of virtue: Reassessing international humanitarianism.* Princeton, NJ: Princeton University Press.

Kenway, J. (2001). Remembering and regenerating Gramsci. In K. Weiler (Ed.), *Feminist engagements: Reading, resisting and revisioning male theorists in education and cultural studies* (pp. 47–65). London: Psychology Press.

Kliebard, H. M. (1975). Bureaucracy and curriculum theory. In W. F. Pinar (Ed.), *Curriculum theorizing: The reconceptualists* (pp. 51–69). Berkeley, CA: McCutchan.

Koerner, M., Lynch, D., & Martin, S. (2008). Why we partner with Teach For America: Changing the conversation. *Phi Delta Kappan, 89*(10), 726–729.

Lack, B. (2009). No excuses: A critique of the Knowledge Is Power Program (KIPP) within charter schools in the USA. *Journal for Critical Education Policy Studies, 7*(2), 126–153.

Laczko-Kerr, I., & Berliner, D. C. (2002, September 6). The effectiveness of "Teach For America" and other under-certified teachers on student academic achievement: A case of harmful public policy. *Education Policy Analysis Archives, 10*(37). Available at: http://epaa.asu.edu/ojs/article/view/316.

Ladson-Billings, G. (1995). But that's just good teaching! The case for culturally relevant pedagogy. *Theory into Practice, 34*(3), 159–165.

Ladson-Billings, G. (2005). Reading, writing, and race: Literacy practices of teachers in diverse classrooms. In T. L. McCarty (Ed.), *Language, literacy, and power in schooling* (pp. 133–150). Mahwah, NJ: Lawrence Erlbaum.

Lather, P. (1991). *Getting smart: Feminist research and pedagogy with/in the postmodern.* New York: Routledge.

LeCompte, M. (1994). Some notes on power, agenda and voice: A researcher's personal evolution toward critical, collaborative research. In P. McLaren & J. Giarelli (Eds.), *Critical theory and educational research* (pp. 91–112). Albany: State University of New York Press.

Lyotard, J. (1979). *The postmodern condition: A report on knowledge.* Minneapolis: University of Minnesota Press.

Lytle, S. (2006). The literacies of teaching urban adolescents in these times In D. Alvermann (Ed.), *Reconceptualizing the literacies in adolescents' lives* (pp. 257–278). Mahwah, NJ: Lawrence Erlbaum.

Macedo, D. (1994). *Literacies of power: What Americans are not allowed to know.* Boulder, CO: Westview.

McAdams, D., & Brandt, C. (2009). Assessing the effects of voluntary youth service: The case of Teach For America. *Social Forces, 88*(2), 945–969.

Miner, B. (2010). The ultimate superpower. *Rethinking Schools, 25*(2), 1–11.

Moll, L. C., Amanti, C., Neff, D., & Gonzáles, N. (2005). Funds of knowledge for teaching: Using a qualitative approach to connect homes and classrooms. In N. González, L. Moll, & C. Amanti (Eds.), *Funds of knowledge: Theorizing practices in households, communities, and classrooms* (pp. 71–88). Mahwah, NJ: Lawrence Erlbaum.

Moll, L., & González, N. (1997). Teachers as social scientists: Learning about culture from household research. In P. Hall (Ed.), *Race, ethnicity and multiculturalism: Vol. 1. Missouri Symposium on and Educational Policy* (pp. 89–114). New York: Garland.

Morrell, E. (2008). *Critical literacy and urban youth.* New York: Routledge.

Morrison, T. (1992). *Jazz.* New York: Knopf.

National Institute of Child Health and Human Development. (2000). *Report of the National Reading Panel. Teaching children to read: An evidence-based assessment of the scientific research literature on reading and its implications for reading instruction* (NIH Publication No. 00-4769). Washington, DC: U.S. Government Printing Office.

Oakes, J., Franke, M. L., Quartz, K. H., & Rogers, J. (2002). Research for high-quality urban teaching: Defining it, developing it, assessing it. *Journal of Teacher Education, 53*(3), 228–234.

Orner, M. (1992). Interrupting the calls for student voice in "liberatory" education: A feminist poststructuralist perspective. In C. Luke & J. Gore (Eds.), *Feminisms and critical pedagogy* (pp. 74–89). New York: Routledge.

Phelan, P., Davidson, A. L., & Yu, H. C. (1997). *Adolescents' worlds.* New York: Teachers College Press.

Polman, L. (2011). *The crisis caravan: What's wrong with humanitarian aid?* London: Picador.

Popkewitz, T. (1998). *Struggling for the soul: The politics of schooling and the social construction of the teacher.* New York: Teachers College Press.

Ravitch, D. (2010). *The death and life of the great American school system: How testing and choice are undermining education.* New York: Basic Books.

Richardson, L. (1997). *Fields of play.* New Brunswick, NJ: Rutgers University Press.

Rist, R. (1970/2000). Student social class and teacher expectations: The self-fulfilling prophecy in ghetto education. *Harvard Educational Review, 70*(3), 266–301.

Rogers, C. R. (2006). "The Turning of One's Soul"—learning to teach for social justice. The Putney Graduate School of Teacher Education (1950–1964). *Teachers College Record, 108*(7), 1266–1295.

Schorr, J. (1993). Class action: What Clinton's national service program could learn from "Teach For America." *Phi Delta Kappan, 75*(4), 315–318.

Shor, I. (1980). *Critical teaching and everyday life.* Boston: South End Press.

Shulman, L. S. (1987). Knowledge and teaching: Foundations of the new reform. *Harvard Educational Review, 51,* 1–22.

Simon, R. (2009). Constructing a language of learning to teach. In M. Cochran-Smith & S. L. Lytle (Eds.), *Inquiry as stance: Practitioner research in the next generation* (pp. 275–292). New York: Teachers College Press.

Sleeter, C. (2005). *Un-standardizing curriculum: Multicultural teaching in the standards-based classroom.* New York: Teachers College Press.

Stearns, J. (2011). *Dancing in the glory of monsters.* New York: Public Affairs.

Street, B. (1984). *Literacy in theory and practice.* Cambridge, UK: Cambridge University Press.

Teach For America. (2007). *Elementary literacy guide.* Teach For America.

Weiler, K. (1991). Freire and a feminist pedagogy of difference. *Harvard Educational Review, 61*(4), 449–474.

Willis, A. I. (1995). Reading the world of school literacy: Contextualizing the experience of a young African American male. *Harvard Educational Review, 65*(1), 30–49.

Wilson, S. M. (1994). *Is there a method in this madness?* (Technical Report CP-94-3). East Lansing, MI: National Center for Research on Teacher Education.

Zeichner, K. (1993). Traditions of practice in U.S. pre-service teacher preparation programs. *Teaching and Teacher Education, 9*(1), 1–13.

Zipin, L. (2009). Dark funds of knowledge, deep funds of pedagogy: Exploring boundaries between lifeworlds and schools. *Discourse: Studies in the Cultural Politics of Education, 30*(3), 317–331.

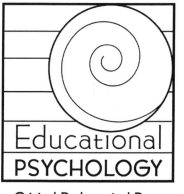

Critical Pedagogical Perspectives

Greg S. Goodman, *General Editor*

Educational Psychology: Critical Pedagogical Perspectives is a series of relevant and dynamic works by scholars and practitioners of critical pedagogy, critical constructivism, and educational psychology. Reflecting a multitude of social, political, and intellectual developments prompted by the mentor Paulo Freire, books in the series enliven the educator's process with theory and practice that promote personal agency, social justice, and academic achievement. Often countering the dominant discourse with provocative and yet practical alternatives, *Educational Psychology: Critical Pedagogical Perspectives* speaks to educators on the forefront of social change and those who champion social justice.

For further information about the series and submitting manuscripts, please contact:

Dr. Greg S. Goodman
Department of Education
Clarion University
Clarion, Pennsylvania
ggoodman@clarion.edu

To order other books in this series, please contact our Customer Service Department at:

(800) 770-LANG (within the U.S.)
(212) 647-7706 (outside the U.S.)
(212) 647-7707 FAX

Or browse online by series at:

www.peterlang.com